MW00909079

Miracles,

Yours For The Asking

♣

Lucille Joyner

♣

Contents

Dedication vii
Introduction ix

Billy, The Kid 11
The Miracle Piano 20
The Dealer 31
The Dead Cat 38
The Chickering Piano 42
A Few Passing Miracles 46
The Prodigal Dad 51
Donna 57
Vision Restored 63
Don't You Trust Me? 68
The Broker 84
The White Supremacist 90
The Poison Case 94
The Stroke 105
The Promised Land 110
    Chapter I   The Little White
                     Church Revisited 110
    Chapter II The Inheritance 133

Chapter III The Addition 139
Chapter IV The Horse 164
Chapter V   The Election 174

Dedication

I dedicate this book to those friends whom God put in my life at crucial times:

Ruth Bangma-Smith saved my life not once, but twice. She, herself, is a living miracle of God. She was told that she had six months to live in 1997 and not only survived terminal cancer after refusing more chemotherapy, but was recently miraculously healed of Hepatitis C that was contracted from a blood transfusion over twenty-five years ago.

Robin Ahlers saved my life by being stubborn. She sat in my kitchen and refused to leave unless I let her bring me to the Emergency Room. It was late and she would not budge. I was forced to let her take me to the hospital, if only to get it over with so I could go to bed. It saved my life. It turned out that *I* was the stubborn one after all.

Honorable Mention goes to those four charitable young women who came to my aid en masse when I most needed it: Janet Rains, Nancy Lord-Alge, Donna Antonow, and Sandi Picard. Their love and kindness meant a great deal to me.

Introduction

*M*iracles, Yours For The Asking is based on my personal diary of observations and experiences over the years from which a pattern emerges that reveals the unmistakable reality of a living God and the Power of Prayer.

Prior to a certain point in my life, there were no miracles. God was up there and I was down here and we could not seem to make contact. In my teens, I embarked on a search for God. There were no answers anywhere, not in the family religion or in any other religion. I couldn't find God anywhere, so I stopped looking.

I married, had children and after twelve years, found myself alone with total support of two children and a house. It was by far the worst period of my life. With this, there were more questions and even fewer answers. I hung on only for the sake of my two innocent children.

Overwhelmed by mounting bills and a sense of hopelessness, I dropped down on the couch one dark day and uttered three words, "Jesus help me!" That's all I had energy for. From that moment on, almost imperceptible changes began to happen. A woman I barely knew called me up out of the blue and said, "God put you on my heart. I have good things to tell you." She introduced me to the Holy Bible, a book that I thought was too sacred to touch, much less open. I found it to be God's Autobiography, written to be read, and not just by those declared holy by sacred systems, but by each and every searching heart. The Bible describes a Living God who is not up there out-of-reach, but right here, waiting to be asked in. Finally, there were answers.

The miracles described in this book are only a few of the highlights. There wouldn't be enough paper to include the everyday miracles, like when an appliance breaks down and you lay hands on it and pray, and it starts back up. Or you are late for an appointment and you pray for a parking space, and one suddenly opens up the minute you get there. Once, a penny dropped into my gear shift while driving and I prayed, and the penny jumped right back out. I had to laugh at that one. Daily miracles are endless.

May you be blessed in reading this book and that it inspires you to believe God for your own miracles.

Billy, The Kid

Just after the birth of my daughter, I wanted to get as far away as possible from the bad neighborhood in Long Island, so we moved to the other side of New York, across the Hudson. The house was bigger and there was more land. This was surely the solution. And the woman who sold us the house lowered the price because she said that God wanted me to have it. She was a very sweet lady, but I didn't take her statement seriously.

Instead of moving to greater peace, we moved into the mouth of an erupting volcano. Directly across the street, there was a home in which both parents worked and their emotionally disturbed preteen son was left without supervision after school. Billy terrorized the whole neighborhood, and since my house was in direct line with his, in fact, it was a mirror image of his house, mine was his most convenient target. Anyone who lived in my house would have to bear the brunt of his pathology.

For five years, Billy's mischief was sporadic because my husband was home a lot. He let up when my husband was around. After our separation, my husband came home weekends to see the children, but during the week, when I was alone, Billy's harassment escalated.

No matter how much I avoided a situation, by the time Billy was in his teens, his mischief turned into crimes. It had evolved from ringing the doorbell and running, to firebombs and damage to my house and car. He also attacked other houses around him, but not as badly as mine. His next door neighbor moved once Billy took their year-and-a-half-old daughter into the woods. He put another boy in the hospital with a rock and the boy had to have a testicle removed. If there ever was a bad seed, Billy was it, and I had to inherit him with that house.

When my husband left the area for Las Vegas, I had no protection at all, and bad situations kept rising up for me to handle. It wasn't enough that I had to struggle to support a household by myself, and had to deal with my children's trauma over the loss of a father, I had to deal with someone else's psychopathic son.

I pleaded with his mother for relief but she was in denial, defending Billy in his most heinous crimes. Her defense of him promoted more delinquency, and the whole neighborhood was ill at ease. Finally, the school authorities forced his mother to quit her job and be home for him because he was doing very bad things in High School. Her rage was worse than his, no doubt where he got it from, and she stomped around the neighborhood angrily, stirring up trouble wherever she could. She must have felt she was at the bottom of the heap, because she was looking for someone to vent her frustration on and, like her son, she focused on the most convenient target in direct line of her house – me. I did nothing more than just happened to live there, and I was so busy working, I had no time or energy for a neighborhood conflict. Sometimes I think that my backing away enraged her more. She wanted to fight with *someone*.

My next door neighbor's husband was in politics and had a lot of connections. The next thing I knew, there was a conspiracy between them and Billy's mother to drive me out of the neighborhood. They all ganged up on me like a school of piranhas diving at a piece of meat. I was totally alone with no one to help me. And I didn't have the money to buy help.

The next thing I knew, the husband next door called me and asked if I had called his wife and hung up. Too bad there wasn't caller ID at the time, because they would have seen that this sort of mischief came from Billy's house, either from him or his mother. I hardly knew these people and had no reason to do such a thing. Since Billy's mother used to go next door, I knew this was her handiwork. And such was that mother's way of life. The more I became aware of this woman's treachery, the more I understood why Billy was the way he was. They were of one mind, always stirring up trouble.

As the neighbor problem was escalating, my husband put someone in the hospital while driving drunk, so he left town in a hurry. I had him put the house in my name to protect it, and since he didn't contribute, I had the worry of carrying everything myself. Without my husband here, Billy had a field day. The first thing he did was to try to put sugar in my gas tank. Fortunately, I had the foresight to put a lock on it, so all he could break was the sliding cover and lose some of the sugar on the garage floor.

His endless attacks took its toll on me. Was it *ever* going to end? Between suddenly having full support of a house and two children, my mimeo machine that brought in extra money broke down the minute the warranty was up and the dealer pulled a fast one and kept my machine. I sold my piano to buy a moped for my son. These neighbors were so convinced that I was making these calls, that the politician next door and the marauders across the street ganged up on me to drive me out of the neighborhood. They tried to scare me by having the police chief question me and a councilman was using my name in a disparaging way in his campaign. I was living on the edge with absolutely no relief in sight. It was at this point that I dropped onto the couch in abject hopelessness and cried, "Jesus, help me!"

Oddly enough, I soon got a call from a woman whom I barely knew—I may have met her in a supermarket or something—who said that God put my name on her mind. She said she had things to tell me, and invited me to breakfast. I said I would go, but I didn't show. I was too depressed to talk to anyone. That day I had a minor car accident that would never have happened had I gone to the woman's house. The next day I went. She told me about Jesus, that He died for our sins, and read beautiful Scriptures to me. And we prayed together. It was such a healing balm to my soul, and it enabled me to think more clearly and work out a plan to save the house.

Ideas began entering my mind. I prepared downstairs for rental in my split level. When I changed the door on the attached garage so roomers could enter that area separately, the building inspector showed up. It was no doubt Billy's mother who called him, but when you have the favor of God, things begin to work out. The building inspector decided to do nothing about my garage door and let everything remain. Not only that, he ended up renting one of the rooms, which put an end to any future complaints by Billy's mother. This might have been the first time the Hand of God intervened. After that, God retrieved my mimeo machine from the crooked dealer, and He brought me a wonderful piano. Things began to look upward.

At the same time, I decided to market my one asset, my musical ear. I had been tuning my own piano for some time, and now it was time to launch a business with it. I was not only tuning pianos, I was also teaching piano after school and typing weekends and summers.

Life was an exhausting whirlwind of work to keep afloat. I brought my children to school, tuned pianos, picked them up, rushed home to teach piano. Billy across the street knew my schedule, and the minute a pupil arrived at my door, he'd dial my telephone number and hang up over and over to disturb the lesson. This was at a time when answering machines were very expensive and were found only in offices.

All you could do was to take the receiver off the hook and have an annoying busy signal in the background. Despite my precarious financial situation, I was forced to buy an answering machine, which opened up a new dimension for Billy. He was now able to leave obscene calls. On one message, his mother called him to dinner in the background, so there was no mistaking who it was. Having such a busy day, then coming home to the misdirected energy of an angry, neglected, and troubled youth and his irrational mother was excruciatingly painful. I did not sleep well and operated solely on nervous energy.

After having prayer with the lady who told me the Good News in the Bible, I began imploring God to do something about the situation. Mysterious things began happening to every single person involved in the conspiracy against me. The police chief, the friend of the next door politician who hauled me into the station for questioning like I was a criminal, was exposed for his crime syndicate connections and was fired. The councilman, who exploited my plight for election purposes, fell off a ladder and broke his arm. Then he lost his license and was thrown out of his union and had to move to another state to work. That was the end of him. The two families that sought to drive me out mysteriously moved one at a time. Billy's family was the first to move. What a blessed day that was! I thanked God over and over as every stick of furniture was loaded into that moving van. Shortly after, the politician and his wife divorced and moved.

It was like God dropped a bomb and they all scattered. I had no idea where everyone went, and I didn't care, just so long as they were out of my life. When they were all gone, a Scripture passed through my mind, that the wicked are in great power, then pass away. "Yea, I sought him but he could not be found," says the Psalmist. That's how I felt when these people were gone. I thanked God for rescuing me from all the evil that was trying to get me on all sides. There were still other challenges, but the worst ones were over.

A few years later, I was sitting alone in a restaurant in between tuning jobs, and the memory of that horrible experience came flooding back. I remember clearly praying, "Lord, I don't understand. You took vengeance on everyone who ganged up on me and brought them all down, all except for the one who started the whole thing."

I wasn't criticizing God, I simply couldn't understand it. His vengeance was upon that whole web of evil people who tried to run me out of town, but He did nothing to the one who started it all. It was a fleeting thought that I put out of my mind.

One day I got a call from my family in another state. My mother had fallen and because of everyone's work schedule, they needed additional help to watch over her. It didn't seem to matter that we were estranged because I had left the family religion in my teens, they needed my help, so they set aside their prejudices.

When I went, my mother was so bruised and in pain that she had not slept in a few days. This day, she finally fell into a deep sleep, and I sat very still in the kitchen so as not to disturb her. There was a newspaper on the table in front of me. I was not at all interested in that newspaper, but I couldn't just sit there and stare at the wall. I opened the paper at random and it opened to the Obituary page. There, in front of my eyes, was the obituary of Billy, that very youth who had brought such pain and suffering to me and my family, not to mention the whole neighborhood. I was shocked! In fact, I didn't believe it. I had to check the names of his parents and sibling before it even registered in my mind. I was stunned! The obit did not say what he died from, but that it was "after a brief illness." Probably drugs, I thought, or maybe someone killed him.

God is so amazing! What are the chances of being in another state and seeing the obituary of a disturbed young troublemaker who brought such pain and suffering to my life? What are the chances of Billy moving to the same state as my mother? What are the chances of his dying at the very time that my mother fell, and his obituary be published on the very day that I had to be there? An obituary is only in the papers one day, and it was on the day that I had to be there. And what are the chances of my opening that paper that I have no interest in and have never opened during any prior visit? It was all too "coincidental" to be a coincidence. Truly . . . as it says in Psalm 37:34: When the wicked are cut off, thou shalt see it.

I never wished death on Billy, just relief from his harassment. I thanked God for the whole experience, because if it hadn't been for the battering I received from these ruthless neighbors, I would have never come to the end of my ways and would never have reached out for God.

Perhaps the seller of the house was right after all when she said that God wanted me to have that house. It was where I found Him.

The Miracle Piano

All the neighborhood boys had a moped, and my son, who had just turned eleven, wanted one, too. As a single parent supporting a house and two children, there was no money for this. We didn't even have furniture and slept on mattresses. The only thing of value was my Yamaha Upright piano. After much soul-searching and with an ache in my heart, I sold the piano. *What difference did it make*? I told myself. *I had no time to play anyway.*

The piano sold for the exact amount of the SL 70, the helmet, and the rest of the riding gear. It was virtually an even trade. While I was happy for my son, I discovered that living without a piano in the house was unbearable. Music kept me together. Even if I had only two minutes a month to play, I needed those two minutes. Without that connection, I felt lost and empty.

My music, my beloved music, became a distant memory. At times, I couldn't even remember ever playing. It was like it was someone else. People always used to ask me, "How old were you when you started playing?" I couldn't remember. I asked my older sister, and she said, "You never began. You just always did."

The piano was an extension of myself, so I didn't have to learn it. I just did it. Music, to me, was my very breath of life, my reason for living.

Was I that same person who boldly called up one of the finest music schools in the world because I wanted to learn to read music? I can still see the professor waving me into his studio and bellowing, "Play!" I walked timidly over to his Steinway B and played Chopin's "Fantasie Impromptu," Beethoven's "Sonata Pathetique," Schumann's "Arabesque," and some Debussy, all music that I had learned from records. He had no idea that I could not read music. My family did not recognize that I was a prodigy. They just thought it was nice that I played, but my father saw no financial value in it, so they never gave it another thought.

When the professor asked how long I had studied, I was too embarrassed to tell him that I never took lessons, so I said, "Two years." In my ignorance, I thought two years was a long time, but it was pitifully short, but what did I know?

I was dumbfounded when he said, "Why don't you apply to the school?" He obviously could not tell that I had never studied. He even complimented me with, "Your phrasing is beautiful." I thanked him, but I didn't know what he was talking about. I had zero understanding of music, yet I asked, "What do I have to do?"

He said, "You have to audition before a panel of judges, and you can play what you just played for me, but it must include at least one Bach Prelude and Fugue."

I had never heard of Bach and he wrote down the recommended edition of the music that I should buy and learn. I did buy it, and also the records of every Prelude and Fugue Bach wrote. I listened to them all, picked out one that appealed to me, and learned it by ear. The professor gave me three lessons, and I let him think that he taught me the Bach Prelude and Fugue. Had the music been upside down on the piano desk, I would not have known the difference. Out of hundreds of applicants from all over the world, only seventeen were accepted, and I was one of the seventeen. Where did all of this go? What happened? How did I go from so much promise to Welfare?

My music remained a painful longing in my heart, but as much as I loved music, I could not put it before the two innocent children that I had willingly brought into the world. I had no idea I would end up with total support. Other than a few piano playing jobs and typing, I had never really had a job before. I was forced to apply for Welfare to feed my children until I could get on my feet.

Life became nothing more than a joyless existence of drudgery and hard work. The loss of my music, the financial struggle while dealing with my children's grief over their father's abandonment, dealing with a psychopathic teenager across the street, losing my mimeograph machine to an old lecher, trying to make ends meet, all served to make life unendurable. I was like a zombie, with each day a little harder than the day before, and no relief in sight. Being a single parent with no family or friends around to help and nowhere to turn was like being on a flimsy raft in the middle of the ocean during a storm. You're always one step away from drowning.

With no child support and a small amount from Welfare, and house bills still coming in, I didn't know which way to turn. Where will the children and I go? Will they end up in an orphanage somewhere? I was so weary, I couldn't think anymore. I dropped down in a depressed hulk on the couch and cried out, "Jesus, help me!"

Scene II

Within a week, a woman I hardly knew called me up and said, "God has put you on my heart." She invited me to breakfast but I didn't show. I was too depressed to see anyone. That day I had a fender-bender and I realized that had I gone to the lady's house, the accident would never have happened. I saw the whole thing as an eerie sign that I should have gone and the next morning I was at the lady's door.

She introduced me to the Bible. It had been years since I went to church and I had never opened a Bible in my life. The Scriptures she quoted began jumping out at me, such as, "You have not because you ask not." I never knew that God wanted us to ask for things. I thought that asking for something was greed, but I reasoned that if God says to do it, it has to be OK, so from this day on, I asked God for a piano—"Not a bad one, Lord, a good one, and, of course, You'd better make it a gift, Lord, because you know I have no money." I don't think a day went by for the next three months that I didn't ask God to bring me a piano of my very own.

Other ideas began coming to me, too. I rented out rooms downstairs in my split level and that covered the mortgage and taxes, and I launched a piano tuning business. I had been tuning my own piano in the past, but now it was time to market this skill. It was a good thing, too, because there were limitations on my time since I had to bring the children to school by nine, and pick them up at three. I was able to earn as much in shorter time in my own business than a full time job would have paid for forty hours a week. Nonetheless, after all bills were covered, I was rich when I had as much as Fifty Dollars left over for the month.

After praying diligently for several months for a piano, reminding God that His Word says to pray till the answer comes, a stranger from New York named Elaine, who got my name from another stranger, called me up. Elaine was moving to Mexico in ten days and said she had a piano to give away. I wondered if this could this be God's answer to my prayer. My budget was so tight that I had second thoughts about spending money for gas and tolls to go look at the piano, not to mention losing time that could be spent earning. Yet, I could not risk missing the answer to my prayer.

I decided to go, and to my utter disappointment, the piano was a bomb. It was a huge painted upright with most of the guts ripped out by her two energetic young sons. It was the sort of piano that you would have to pay someone to dump. I was disheartened. As I was leaving, I turned to wish her well in her new venture. I noticed a huge shadow in a side room.

"What is that, another piano?"

"Yes," she answered, "that's my Steinway."

"Oh. I suppose you're taking that one with you?"

"No, I'm selling it. I've placed an Ad in the New York Times and it will be coming out Sunday, tomorrow."

"Really? What are you asking for it?"

"Four hundred dollars."

"Four hundred dollars?" There was a twinge in my heart. A Steinway for that price was unheard of at *any* time in history.

"You'll have no problem selling it. I'll bet you get thirty to forty calls."

I was upset that I was in no position to take advantage of such a once-in-a-lifetime opportunity but all I had to my name was Fifty Dollars.

She gave me permission to play it, and as I slid down to the bench, I said, facetiously, "Let me know when you come down to Three Hundred." That was a laugh, because I couldn't raise Three Hundred any more than I could raise Four.

The piano was a Professional Upright from the early 1900's and it had a tone that was beautiful beyond words. I had never played a piano so fine before. Between the rich resonant bass and a crystal clear treble, playing it was ethereal, like being transported to a celestial realm. As I played, something supernatural was happening, something I had never experienced before. An unexplainable warmth began traveling through my hands and arms until it permeated my whole body. My music became a personal prayer language, as though I was playing in tongues before God. While I did not hear audible words, I knew deep in my spirit that this piano was mine. It made no sense whatsoever, yet I knew that I knew, and a sense of excitement welled up in me.

I didn't want to impose on Elaine by playing too long, so I tore myself away from this magnificent instrument and said goodbye. All the way home, I was beside myself with joy. I found myself thanking God over and over for such an exquisite piano. My joy would suddenly be rudely interrupted with, "What's the matter with you? Are you dreaming? This piano will be in the New York Times tomorrow and there's no way it won't be snatched up." I could see people ruthlessly bidding on it against each other, stepping over each other's body to get that piano. Yet, I knew the piano was mine. It made no sense whatsoever.

Even if she didn't get a buyer, which was highly unlikely, there was no way I could raise the money. Despite all the logical arguments against my having that piano, I could not shake the deep sense that this piano was mine. Sunday came and went and I tried to be realistic, telling myself that the piano surely must be sold by now. At the same time, I was looking around the house for the best spot to put it.

That Friday, six days after I looked at it, the phone rang. It was Elaine. I was so surprised, I could hardly speak. Why would she be calling me . . . unless . . . could it be? Then I heard the words, words that I had been dreaming of, "Do you still want the piano?" I was so taken aback, I couldn't answer. She had to repeat herself several times, then added, "... and you can have it for Three Hundred. Do you still want it?"

My mind was whirring with excitement when I blurted out, "Of course, of course, but. . ."

"If you can get it out by tomorrow, it's yours. I will be leaving for Mexico in four days and there's no time to re-advertise and the landlord says that if I leave anything in the apartment, he will keep my security. Do you want the piano?"

"Of course I want the piano, but I don't understand. What happened? Didn't it come out in the New York Times Sunday?"

"Yes, it did, and you were right. Over thirty people called and I scheduled them all for Thursday, yesterday. I took the day off from work to sell the piano and to dispose of the rest of my furniture, and the strangest thing happened. Yesterday, New York had the worst electrical storm in its entire history, and *not one person showed up.*"

Words cannot describe the impact these words had on me. *"Not one person showed up."* It was like watching the Red Sea open. It is one thing to believe in God, but it's another thing to experience God.

I finally spoke, "Not one person? Didn't you take down anyone's name or number?"

"No, I didn't. I should have, but I didn't, and I've got to get this piano out of here or I lose my security."

Almost too overwhelmed to speak, I said, "Yes! I want the piano! But wait a minute! We're forgetting one thing here. I don't have Three Hundred Dollars."

"Get a pencil," she ordered, "and take this down." She dictated an address to me and said, "When you have the money, send it to that address." Incredibly, she was as anxious to get the piano out of her life as I was to get it into mine. She was even willing to trust a perfect stranger for the money.

After counting out the Fifty Dollars that I had set aside for emergencies, I called a piano mover that I had been dealing with in my business, and he was willing to pick up the piano for me the next day. You would think this was the end of the miracle, but it wasn't. It rippled on.

The next day, in the morning mail, a check came from my late father's estate for the exact amount of the piano, Three Hundred Dollars. There was no explanation, just a check with his business name on it. I couldn't call my family because they wrote me off when I left the family religion years earlier, so I was left wondering about that check. Within the year, at a family funeral, I asked the Executrix about the check and she said she didn't know what I was talking about, that she had no recollection of sending me a Three Hundred-Dollar check. Puzzled, I asked my sisters and brothers about the check, and no one else in the family received a check or knew anything about it. Since the Executrix and family members had no knowledge of a Three Hundred Dollar check, I can only conclude, and am convinced, that God simply materialized the check to complete the answer to my prayer. What other explanation can there be?

I cashed it and sent the money with the movers to pay Elaine for the piano. Before the day was over, the magnificent treasure—the Steinway Professional Upright—was in my home, in that very space that was chosen for it. For the next few days, I had to keep touching it every time I went by it to see if it was really there, that it wasn't a dream.

That evening, I was at a Piano Technicians meeting, and I was so excited about the piano, I told the tuner next to me about my prize, the Steinway Professional Upright. He asked, "How much did you pay for it?" I answered, "Three hundred." Without batting an eyelash, he said, "I'll give you Nine." Sight unseen, this technician was willing to give me triple, that's how good the piano was.

Even though I still had very little time to play, the Miracle Piano stood there as a tribute to a God who cares and who answers prayers.

Coda: This miracle piano was my first step out of the hell I was in. The money from giving piano lessons supplemented my income from the downstairs tenants and my growing piano tuning business. I was now able to support the household adequately, but I had spent so much of my early life at the piano, I didn't understand things. I had no idea how to get off Welfare. I hated to lie, but I wanted to get this

Welfare thing off my back. I wrote them a letter and told them that my husband had decided to resume child support, so I won't need the Welfare checks any longer. They probably went into shock. I'm sure they don't get requests like this very often.

Between watching God resolve my major problem by giving me such a marvelous piano, and ridding the neighborhood of the delinquent, and getting my mimeo machine back, life was turning around. I could see the light at the end of the tunnel, and that light was God.

The Dealer

The piano business is slow in the summer when school is out. Piano lessons stop, people go away on vacation, and the piano becomes just another piece of furniture. However, my expenses do not stop. With total support of two minor children, I had to find work at home so that I could not only make up the lost income, but be at home for my children. I accomplished my goal by doing typing and mimeographing.

Just before I accepted the Lord, I was working on a mimeographing job for a school enrichment program. I pressed the ON button on the mimeograph machine and it stuck. I needed an emergency repair to finish the job, so I looked up the closest authorized dealer I could find. It was a hot summer day, and it took every bit of strength and energy I had to carry this heavy machine to my car, drive half an hour, and carry it into the store.

The dealer was a huge man named Marty who sat at a desk with a lit cigar in one hand and a telephone receiver in the other. He was shouting threats at someone and with a few choice expletives, he slammed the receiver down. I remember his booming voice as he angrily spat out what he was going to do to that person. I was sorry I went there, but it was too much for me to carry this machine back out and look for another place. This was the closest authorized dealer I could find and I was already there. I couldn't wait to get my business over with in this place and leave.

I asked the dealer how much it would be to fix the ON switch, and he said, "No more than forty dollars," so I left the machine with him. Then I asked him if there was a restaurant nearby. I hadn't eaten all day and I was feeling very weak. I needed a little something before the drive home.

The man surprised me with, "Right around the corner. Wait, I'll go with you," and he locked up the store and walked with me to the restaurant. I was very uncomfortable with this man but I didn't want to be rude.

After a short time in the restaurant, the dealer made an indecent proposal. My BLT stopped in mid-air. I couldn't believe my ears. I hadn't said or done anything to invite such a proposal and I refused him as gently as I could, but he became enraged. In fact, he became so angry that he stopped speaking to me and stomped out of the restaurant ahead of me. I trailed behind to get back to my car.

A few days later, the dealer called me and said, "Your machine is ready. That'll be one hundred and ninety dollars . . ."

I gasped. It was obvious that it wasn't repairs that ran up this bill; it was his wounded ego. The machine was new, just barely out of warranty.

". . .and the machine will sit here until you pay!" he barked, in his customary telephone etiquette.

I didn't have that kind of money so he, in effect, put me out of business. I explained the situation to the woman whose job I could not finish, and she was very understanding. Gina was such a kind, compassionate human being who was always concerned about my children and me. She did her best to farm out her organization's work to me to give me more income.

The dealer's cruelty added to the mounting pressures that broke me when I cried out, "Jesus, help me!" that day on the couch. After committing my life to God, I fully expected that God would touch someone in my small home church to come forward and help me retrieve my machine. No help was forthcoming. I began to wonder what happened. Wasn't He hearing my prayers? Doesn't He know that I need the income from this mimeo machine?

No matter how many miracles God performs for us, our faith, particularly at the beginning of our Christian walk, seems to give way if we don't get an immediate answer. In my precarious situation, having total physical and emotional support of two small children, I was often physically and mentally exhausted from the strain of overwork and overwhelming responsibility. This may have contributed to my wavering faith.

Gina called me from time to time to see if I had my machine back and after five months she said, "This is ridiculous! I'll have my husband call you. He's a lawyer." I fully expected God to have another believer help me, but He had other plans. He chose a Jewish Atheist. The first miracle here was that the Lawyer took a Friday off from his New York practice to help me. When does a lawyer ever do that? After a little preliminary work, he called and said, "Lucille, let's go get your machine."

I couldn't understand why believers had ignored my plight while an Atheist with compassion came forward. Is compassion an individual trait that is detached from religious belief? We can question all we want, but God knows what He's doing. It was I who had to learn about the perfect way in which God does things. He does answer every prayer, and He answers in the best possible way and at the best possible moment. And God uses whomever He will to do it.

Even though a lawyer was willing to help me, I still had to raise money to get the machine. Needless to say, my incessant prayers beat on the doors of Heaven for that money. Only days before we were to go get the machine, I received a letter from a southern Pastor/Tuner whom I hardly knew, I think I met him at a meeting, who said that he felt led by God to send me a check. That was the first and only time in our brief business relationship that he ever did this and today I can't even remember his name. Another check came from my mother out of the clear blue. She had a 'feeling' she said. Also, I still had my original forty dollars. By the time we went to get the machine, I had more than enough.

I will never forget the ride to the dealer. This lawyer—who looked like Kojak, bald and bold— had 'presence.' He was the sort of person who, if he walked into a room, would immediately have everyone's attention. He radiated power and authority.

"Don't say a word," he cautioned. "I'll do the talking."

It was painful to walk into that store again, much like returning to the scene of a crime. However, a strange thing happened. While the dealer was a fearsome Goliath when he dealt with me, he became a cowering yes-man with this lawyer. I almost laughed aloud as I saw him shrinking before my eyes. He was very brave around a 5-foot-2 hundred pound woman, but he was a sniveling coward around a 6-ft powerful New York lawyer.

The lawyer checked the itemized list that he had previously requested of the dealer, and even with all the bogus services that were listed, he could not bring the bill up to $190.00. With a fictional cleaning and imaginary replaced parts, he could not stretch it past $168.00. Even so, this was a high figure at the time. I'm not sure the machine cost too much more than that.

We paid him to the penny and my last memory of this cigar-totin' bully was his huffing and puffing as he lugged the machine to our car. It ultimately cost me no more than the initial forty dollars that he quoted. Of course, I lost all of the money I could have made during the time he held my machine, but God later made it up to me.

The lawyer then drove to the manufacturer where some representatives were awaiting us. I didn't know that the lawyer had set this up. They opened and examined my mimeo machine and checked it against the itemized bill. From the glances they gave each other, they knew it was a bogus bill. I was just happy that I had the machine back. I immediately discharged the whole matter by praying for the dealer and putting the whole thing behind me.

A few months later, the salesman from whom I bought my mimeo ink appeared at my door. This man had been rebuilding a piano in his spare time and whenever I bought ink from him, I'd help him as much as I could by giving him piano parts and telling him what to do. He was now leaving the mimeo supplies business and had a carload of samples to get rid of, so he brought them to me. Supplies were not cheap, so this was God's way of reimbursing me for my financial loss from lost mimeo work.

After piling the supplies in my front hall, he said, "Did you hear what happened to the dealer?"

I said, "No, what happened?"

"The company withdrew their product from him and that put him out of business."

My jaw dropped open. In other words, the way he put me out of business, the company put *him* out of business—just after they inspected the machine and his bogus bill.

"And his partnership dissolved," the man continued.

I was trying to interpret what I was being told in relation to God's Word in Psalm 37:34 that says, "When the wicked are cut off, you shall see it." God's vengeance was on this cruel man and the results came right to my door so I could see it. I was in awe.

But there's more. Around five years after the bogus bill issue, I happened to attend a prayer meeting on the very street where the dealer lived. When I mentioned his name, they said, "Oh yes, we remember him. He no longer lives here. Four or five years ago his wife divorced him and the house was sold. I think he moved to Florida."

When God says, "The vengeance is mine!" He sure means it. By defrauding a struggling mother who was desperately trying to earn money to support her children, the dealer brought God's vengeance on his head. Not only did he lose his partner and his business, but his marriage and his house, also. In effect, he lost everything.

I used to be angry for days whenever people cheated me. While there will always be a feeling of disappointment on a human level, it is now superseded by concern for them. If you can look past the physical to the spiritual, you can see that cruel people automatically trigger God's vengeance on their heads. It may not happen immediately, so they think they've gotten away with something, but their days are numbered. The wheels of God's justice are sometimes slow, but they are sure.

The Dead Cat

I always thought that asking God for something was a sign of greed, that we had to accept the philosophy of the tune "Che Sera, Sera" or "Whatever will be will be." With this philosophy, we are all corks in the ocean, blown about by any ill wind that comes along. Life just takes us where it will, and there's nothing we can do about it.

Then I was introduced to the Bible and two Scriptures, in particular, changed my thinking. One is Matt 16:24 "Ask and you will receive . . And the other is." Matt 19:26 "With God, all things are possible." Knowing these two Scriptures is enough to move heaven and earth. We don't even have to accept what we see before our very eyes. Through prayer, God can change things.

My newfound faith was put to the test when a neighbor called one morning to tell me that our cat was hit by a car and that she moved the carcass to the side of the road. I was very distressed at this news, as the children had been through enough trauma in their young lives, and the love of this pet was an important consolation for them. It lay there all day until mid-afternoon when my children came home from school. They burst through the front door screaming and crying.

Instead of calling the town to pick up the cat, we had a different approach. The children and I used a towel as a stretcher and brought the cat indoors. The cat was absolutely mangled, with intestines showing out the back end and one leg separated from it's body, it's mouth open with a dry tongue hanging down. We put a mirror up to its mouth. Nothing.

I consoled the children with, "Don't worry, God brought Lazarus back from the dead after four days, He can surely bring back a dead cat after only half a day."

As the cat lay motionless in our foyer, the children and I laid hands on it and I prayed, "Breathe Your breath of life into this little cat, Oh Lord." I particularly remember saying, "Lord God, I know You love little children and mine are inconsolable. They have lost their father, please don't have them lose their pet, too. You have the power of Life and Death, and I know You are a merciful God. Please heal this cat, in Jesus' name. Amen."

Before we could get to the "Amen," The cat startled us by opening its eyes and giving out one meow, then passing out. At least it was alive, now, but I didn't know what to do next. He was in such bad shape. We wrapped him in the towel and placed him gently in front of the refrigerator where there was a steady flow of warm air from the motor to keep the cat comfortable all night. We did our part, we prayed. Now it was up to God.

The following morning, I could see that though the cat was alive, he wasn't able to do much more than lie there. I knew he had to have water, so we laid hands on him and prayed for him to take in water, and we put a dish of water near him. We could see from the water level that he was drinking. I knew that once water went in one end, it had to come out the other, but that he was too incapacitated to use a litter box. We relocated the cat to the bathtub where we made up a cozy bed at one end and hoped that the drain could be used as a litter box, but there was a problem. The poor cat tried to accommodate, but he couldn't. He must have been hit in the backside, because there was a blockage, so we laid hands on the cat again and prayed that the intestines would withdraw into the body, back where they belonged. Little by little, he was able to function. The cat now drank water freely and was able to eliminate. Soon he would be ready for food.

Each day, the cat was a little stronger and was eating more and more, but there was one major problem. The rear leg was detached at the hip, obviously where he was hit by the car, so that when he tried to walk to his food dish, you could see that the leg was not connected. What good would it be if the cat ate and drank, but couldn't walk, so we laid hands on the hip and asked God to reattach the leg. The next thing we knew, the leg was firmly back in place.

It isn't as if the healing took place instantly before our eyes. We would lay hands on him, pray, then wrap the cat up and put him in his bed and leave it to God to do the miracle. We prayed, trusting that God would work on it, and we went about our business. Then the next time we checked the cat, it would be accomplished. Soon, the leg was supporting the body and the cat was walking properly. It seemed that God relied on our faith step by step to complete the total healing. Children have the most incomprehensible faith, so there was no doubt in their minds that God would revive and restore their cat.

I often thought about what would have happened had we brought the cat to a vet. First of all, God knew our finances. I didn't have the money to pay for medical care for the family, much less for a cat, so that would have been reason enough not to go. And I am sure the vet would have looked at us quizzically, wondering why we have placed a dead cat on his examining table. And I can't imagine what the cost of the surgery to reattach the leg would have been.

It took about a week or two of concentrated, steady prayer for this dead, mangled cat to walk briskly to the front door, meowing loudly to go out. However, we did not let him out after this experience.

We took God at His Word. We asked. He answered.

The Chickering Piano

It was Saturday morning and it was such a hard week, I didn't have the energy to get out of bed. I just lay there in a fatigued heap, praying and thinking, thinking of what a mess my life was. I would have been happy to die that moment because life was too painful, with nothing but work and more work, and no relief in sight.

I felt resentment for an ex-husband who ran from responsibility and was living the high life in Las Vegas behind an unlisted number while the children and I were struggling week after week trying to make ends meet. I wondered what I could possibly have done to him to warrant such cruelty. I was angry that his abandonment left the children traumatized and with needs that made demands beyond my capabilities and physical strength. On top of all that, for the first time ever, I had an insurance bill coming up and didn't have the money to pay it, nor did I have the strength to work more than I was already working. I prayed for energy to get up so I could give the children breakfast.

Right in the middle of my self-destructive reverie, a woman called my name and entered the room. It was Helen. To this day, I don't know how she got into the house as my children had not left their rooms yet, and the front door was certainly locked for the night.

Helen stood at my bedside and said, "Get up, Lucille, and get the children ready. You're coming with us." I was in such a defeated mood, I didn't have an opinion left, nor did I care where we were going. What difference did it make, anyway? She was a decent person, so it couldn't be anyplace bad.

Helen and Ernie's son, Eddie, was a change-of-life baby, so while our sons were the same age, they were a good twenty years older than I. They were in the antique business and had the most intriguing and colorful collection of items that made their house look like a storybook fantasy. Dolls, and clocks, and toys, and marble-top tables, and velvet chairs, all different, yet all seemed to belong. Every item had beauty and history and going there was like visiting a museum. The dolls were so lifelike that I wondered if they came to life at midnight with song and dance and returned to their frozen state at dawn.

Recently, Helen and Ernie had ignored my protests and forced some very nice bedroom sets on us. It didn't bother me at all that we were sleeping on mattresses on the floor, but it apparently bothered them. They wouldn't take no for an answer, but I let the furniture in only after they agreed to put a price tag on it so I could one day pay them for it.

I knew that whatever Helen had in mind for this day, it had something to do with an auction or a garage sale. That's the business they were in. I just didn't understand what it had to do with me. Why were they bringing me there? I got up, got the kids ready, and we were on our way in their car. They took us to a mansion in which all contents were being auctioned off.

On the way in, we put our coats on a piano that was covered with a mound of coats. I had to move a few coats to see the name. It was a Chickering Grand and it appeared to be in good shape. If this is why they brought me here, it's out of the question. I didn't have the money, but they told me not to worry about it.

The piano was the very last thing to be auctioned off in this mansion, and by now, most of the people were gone. Ernie bid $200, and someone else bid $225. Then Ernie bid $250 and that person dropped out. It was over in a minute and this top brand piano was ours for the unbelievable price of $250, unheard of for a grand piano in good shape at any time. They did this for me and were going to move it to my house, but I told them it would never sell from there. My house was bare and this beautiful grand needed to be in a well-decorated setting. They agreed to take it to their house and it looked beautiful surrounded by ornate antiques.

The piano was in such excellent shape, I only had to clean it, tighten it up, do a few routine things, and tune it. God was in this situation, because almost immediately, it sold for $2,200. First, I paid Helen and Ernie for the bedroom sets, the piano, and the piano move. Then I paid all of my bills, the insurance, the mortgage, everything, and with the balance, the children and I went to a Chinese restaurant. It had been such a long time since we went out to a restaurant. It was a real treat for them.

This Chickering Grand miracle showed me that God knew what I was going through and he answered my desperate prayer. I did not know many other believers at this time, so I always prayed alone. In time, there were prayer partners, and that multiplied the power for even greater miracles.

A Few Passing Miracles

New York Parking

Once, I had to do a piano in New York City at a Jazz Historical place, and it was on 57th St, I believe. I dreaded it because I knew there would be a parking problem and I didn't feel like circling for two hours, then spending a fortune for a parking garage.

When I got there, I prayed that God would open up a space right away, and just as I prayed someone pulled out of a choice spot right across the street from where I had to go. As I was crossing the street, the policeman that was directing traffic said, "Lady, that was a miracle." As I passed, I answered smugly, "I know it."

The Pump

There were torrential rains in town and everyone's basement had at least a foot or more of water. It was so bad that firemen were called in to pump out people's basements. I didn't need their help since I had a sump pump in the basement. To my utter chagrin, after refusing town help, I found that the pump didn't work. I had at least 5" of water and it wasn't going anywhere.

I did everything I could to get the pump to work, changed the position of the pump, turned the switch on and off, smacked the pump with a lead pipe in case of blockage, but nothing worked.

Then I called a neighbor in, and he took the switch apart and tightened everything, and said that the switch was OK, but that didn't help. The pump still didn't work.

Discouraged, I looked around at the terrible mess that the water had caused. Everything stored in boxes was ruined and important papers were floating in the water. It was a disaster.

I finally did what I should have done in the first place. I laid hands on the pump and began praying, "Lord, God, You see the fix that I'm in and You know I don't have the money for a repairman. Please . . ." and before I could finish the prayer, there was a loud suction sound and the pump was working. After a moment of shock, I grabbed a push broom and helped direct the water toward the pump.

The Gas Gauge

There was a gas shortage and you could not get gas unless your gas gauge pointed to half a tank or less. This created a lot of stress since I had limited work hours. I had to bring my children to school by 9:00 AM and pick them up at 3:00 PM and work in between. Things were hard and I couldn't lose work sitting in gas lines. I didn't know what to do, so I prayed for God to help me.

Miraculously, my gas gauge stuck on Empty and stayed that way for the duration of the shortage, so I was able to get gas easily, at any time. When the gas emergency was over, the gas gauge sprung back to normal.

The Muffler

I was driving along a one lane main road with the mother of the driver of the car ahead. The daughter knew the directions and we were following her. I forget where we were going, but as we were moving along, we noticed that the muffler dropped down from her car. It didn't break loose but dragged along, causing bright sparks to fly all over the road. The daughter was unaware of her dilemma, and was zipping right along. There was absolutely no way that we could pass or signal her daughter, and the mother became alarmed. I said, "Let's pray."

We did, and the muffler jumped right back in place and stayed.

The Ice

My house was at least 500 ft from the road and there came what was described as the worst snow storm in fifty years. It was a little nerve wracking to be locked in since I knew that with the slant in the upper part of the driveway, not even an emergency vehicle could make it to my door.

I decided to try to get out to stock up on groceries since I would be house bound. The snow was deep, but soft, so I managed to get my car out going downhill, but when I came back, it was touch-and-go trying to get up that incline. I'd go up and slide right back down. It took a long time, but when I finally got to the top, I tried to park by my deck, but it was hopeless. The snow drifts were too deep and I was getting stuck in the grooves I was making. Finally, I had to leave the car away from the house, but at least pointing downhill. Walking gingerly from my car to the deck, I figured I could somehow get my car downhill if necessary. Gravity was on my side.

It happened that though the rain had brought the snow level down, that night, everything that melted turned to ice. I absolutely needed food and needed to mail a bill out, so I made the perilous walk to my car, slipping and sliding over all the ruts and grooves that were caused when I tried to bring the car close to the house.

What I found was that the car was immoveable; tires spun and nothing budged. I was so sorry that I did not keep my car down below where the driveway was level. Now I was in trouble. No matter how many times I tried, it was useless. The weather report was bad and I knew that if I didn't get out, I was going to be marooned in my house.

All my efforts did nothing but make the tires go deeper into the ice. The wheels spun until they smoked. I should have given up at this point and just slide carefully back to the house, but I remembered that I did everything except pray.

Exhausted as I was, I prayed, "God, I have to get out and only You can help me. Please send angels to lift this car over the ice so I can get down to the road. I pray in Jesus' Name, amen." I knew that I knew that God would answer my prayer.

I started up the car, barely touched the pedal, and I could feel the car going up and over the ice grooves. It was such a miracle to find myself on the road to do my errands, and, of course, when I returned, I parked down below so that I could get in and out easily.

The Prodigal Dad

My daughter was 5 and my son, 10, when their father disappeared behind an unlisted phone number in Las Vegas. It was initially an amicable split and, in fact, we drove him to the airport when he left the area. Once there, everything changed.

As a musician, he had been away from home for periods of time, so the children thought this was just another trip. They waited, and waited, and waited for his return, and when they finally realized that he wasn't coming back, I could see a steady, almost imperceptible daily change in their personalities. It was as though the very heart was ripped out of them and each day was a little heavier and sadder than before. I truly believe that abandonment is a form of slow-motion murder.

My daughter first tried everything a 5 year old could think of to bring him back. She would set a place for him at the dinner table, thinking he would then have to show up. But she would end up staring wistfully at his empty plate. In time, her tears turned to silence, and she became very quiet, depressed. My son, on the other hand, became angry at the world. He went from a gifted honor student to barely passing, leaving a trail of destruction, like a tornado.

As the years went by, my daughter's need for her father became acute, almost obsessive. Whenever she'd see a man carrying a musical instrument, she'd walk up to him and ask, "Do you know my father? He plays trombone." She reminded me of the little match girl.

One day I told her, "God can do anything. He can bring you and your father together. Why don't we pray about it?" So we agreed in prayer everyday for a year. Nothing changed and my daughter became very depressed. That summer a nearby college was offering a jazz program for high school musicians. Even though her father was Big Band and I was Classical and Jazz, and my daughter was Rock, she agreed to go to the Jazz program. She would be able to stay on campus and meet musicians her own age. The program was designed to give high school students a taste of college life. I was hoping it would be a distraction from her pain.

She liked it and wanted to go a second week. On the weekend between sessions, she and I went to look at a summer camp in New England. On the way back, we stopped to see some people who had been neighbors when her father was with us. In fact, they are the ones who installed the sliding glass door on our house. I forgot that they took pictures of the children's father in front of the new slider. My daughter was very excited over the pictures and she pressed them for every detail about her father. She had such a thirst to know everything about him and she questioned and questioned them.

In the drive home, there was heaviness in the air. We were both stirred by the concentrated reminiscence of her father, and neither one of us spoke for most of the trip. Finally, she broke the silence with, "Mom, God doesn't hear us. I'm not going to pray anymore." I said nothing, but my heart was heavy. I understood how she felt. When we got home and I was alone before God, I was so unhappy, I couldn't pray. The best I could manage was to blurt out "God! Do something!" Like my daughter, I assumed He wasn't listening.

The summer program consisted of classes during the day, and Jazz concerts at night. That Thursday night, her second week there, she was very depressed and didn't want to go to the concert. Another student talked her into going. When she entered the concert hall, there was a famous Jazz trombonist, Bill Watrous, and his band playing. She walked up to him on the bandstand and said, "Do you know my father? He plays trombone, too. I haven't seen him in nine years."

Bill Watrous asked, "What's his name?"

She told him, and he said, "What? He's my best friend . . . and he's sitting right over there."

He called a short break and walked my daughter over to her father, but before Bill could even open his mouth, she and her father flew into each other's arms. Nine years hadn't changed a thing. They knew each other.

She had a good ten-twelve-year relationship with him before he died, and it changed her life. It, in effect, rescued her.

<u>CODA</u>: Because I don't like questioning children, it took years for me to piece together the sequence of events that occurred from the day we first started praying for the miraculous reunion. While it seemed like God was doing nothing, He was working on it the instant the prayers left our lips.

First of all, when my husband first went to Las Vegas, his great credentials got him the best job available in music, Relief Band. He had been with Tommy Dorsey, Benny Goodman, and once off the road, he was on staff at CBS for ten years, so he was well-qualified for a top position in Las Vegas. With a new job and plenty of money, he discarded all prior responsibilities and severed all ties with the past.

What happened to him makes me even more certain that when people do bad or dishonorable things, there are consequences. After two years of high living in Las Vegas, he was backing up a Sammy Davis Jr. show when he suddenly lost control of the horn. The dentist could find nothing wrong with his teeth. His doctor could find nothing wrong with his health, but sent him to a Neurologist to check out his facial nerves. His doctor then had him x-rayed for a brain tumor. He even went for acupuncture, to no avail. In other words, *there wasn't a thing wrong with him, but he no longer could play his horn.* It was the end of life as he knew it. I often wondered if losing his gift was

God's judgment on him for abandoning his innocent children.

After losing the best Vegas job in music, his life spiraled downward through non-music jobs until all he could find was a job as security guard. He was a lost soul without his music. That's how I felt when he took my music from me by giving me such a heavy burden in life, and now his was taken from him.

When my daughter and I first started our prayer vigil, a musician passed through Las Vegas and told him that there was plenty of work in Atlantic City, where the musical standards were not as high as Las Vegas. There was a glimmer of hope that he could play again, so he began making preparations to relocate to Atlantic City.

It took as long as we prayed to make arrangements to move across country. Meanwhile, he and Bill Watrous were in touch with each other right along. Then Bill gets the call to play the Jazz concert at the college not far from us, and he calls the children's father in Atlantic City and invites him to come to the concert. Then I do the unthinkable and book my daughter in a Jazz program at that college when she knows nothing and cares nothing about Jazz. I did it to get her mind off her father, never dreaming that the college would be the very place where she would meet him.

God was weaving an intricate tapestry with all the threads coming together in a perfect work of art. All of this took at least a year. It's a big move from Las Vegas to Atlantic City, involving apartment leases, getting rid of excess furniture, and finding a new apartment, U-Hauling across country, so while we saw nothing for a year on this end, God was working out all the details on the other end.

We lost hope only four days before the answer manifested, but God didn't rescind the answer just because we gave up. The prayer was already answered the first time we prayed, and nothing was going to stop the momentum, not even our waning faith at the end.

The proof that this huge relocation was brought about for the sole purpose of bringing my daughter and her father together was the fact that there was no work in music available in Atlantic City after all. *It turned out to be just a rumor,* and after six months, when he saw that there was no work for him there, he returned to Las Vegas. But now the door was open for a relationship with his daughter, who traveled back and forth to Las Vegas to enjoy both of us.

There is no limit to what God will do to bring about an answer to our prayers. Even when we think He's not listening or is not interested, He's working on it.

Vision Restored

W hen I was a child, I was ashamed of my Mother. She wasn't like other mothers. For one thing, I was her change-of-life baby, the last of nine, so she was actually old enough to be my grandmother while all the other kids had young mothers. She also was from another culture and spoke broken English. She wore these black shoes with the square heel—Nuns shoes, I called them—that made a clumping sound when she walked. She carried a big black pocketbook with many compartments, her hand-held file cabinet.

Underneath her cotton housedress was a petticoat. She was like a Brinks armored car, because in that petticoat were sewn many pockets in which she kept her money and valuables. It was so heavy, that if it ever dropped, I was sure it would end up on the floor below.

My childhood was a lonely time. With all those family members, there wasn't one that I could go to with a problem. I felt like an orphan. As I grew, I searched for answers, leaving the family religion.

After that, with the exception of my mother and my mentally-challenged sister, no one would speak to me. If they had let me explore, I would have gone full circle and returned to the family religion down the line, but because they were so harsh, I could not return even when I came full circle.

My mother's life was hard. She had every baby possible, and in between, every miscarriage possible, and she worked from dawn to dusk. My father, despite his success in business, kept her on the same paltry allowance of their poorer days. He had no conscience about seeing her work so hard though he had the means to provide help for her. Basically, we were all poor children of a rich father. My mother sought solace in prayer.

One day, my mother cried out to God for help. That night she dreamed that Jesus walked over to her and handed her a piece of paper. She said, "What do I want with this, Jesus?" and she threw it on the floor. When she looked down, she saw that the paper had opened up and on it were three numbers. The next day, she kept thinking about those numbers. She felt they had meaning, so she played the lottery. She won!

She bought an income-producing building, then that one bought another, and life changed. I was a child prodigy and music was my passion. She upgraded from an old upright piano to a grand, and gave me a large weekly allowance so I didn't have to walk around like a ragamuffin anymore. Still, I couldn't get rid of that irrational longing for a "real" mother who understood things, someone I could talk to.

It took many experiences in life to realize that there *is* no perfection on earth. Nobody's mother is perfect, no matter where they were born, or where they were educated, or if they were educated, or how much money they had. A change in attitude was slowly developing in me over the years, especially when I saw that my mother was growing old. I wasn't ready to lose her just when I was discovering her, so when she was 87, I prayed, "God, please give her three more years. She is the one person on earth who loves me unconditionally and I can't lose her just yet." God heard. As she was turning 90, I prayed, "Lord, I'm renewing the contract with you. I'm still not ready to lose my mother. Please give her another three years." God heard. When she was 93, I renewed the contract once again, and again at 96. I couldn't give her up. And God heard.

When she was approaching 99, I was tempted to renew the contract with God, but I had reservations. She was living with a sister who worked all day and did not like being tied down nights and weekends. My mother was not sick or disabled and paid for a woman to sit with her days, but my sister found it too nerve-racking to work all day, then be housebound nights and weekends. She knew that you couldn't just go off and leave my mother alone. I wanted my mother with me, but she wouldn't move two hours away.

The last time I visited my mother, she was distressed because the ophthalmologist took care of the cataract on one eye only and she couldn't see out of the other, so I asked, "Why did they do only one eye?"

"The doctor said that the other eye was too old."

I said, "Too old? Aren't your eyes the same age?"

I said, "Mama, do you want me to pray for your eyes? God can do anything. Sarah in the Bible was your age when God gave her a baby."

My mother thought about that, then said, "Gee, I hope He doesn't do that to me." She was a pro at one-liners. To this day, I don't know whether she knew what she was saying, or it just came out that way. She might have been putting us all on right along.

Even though she wasn't sure what religion I was, it didn't seem to matter by this time, so she let me pray for her—first time ever. I laid hands on her eyes and asked God to restore her sight. It was a precious moment between us. All of the silent criticisms of her from my childhood disappeared. We were united under the same God and our souls met. I could feel the presence of the Holy Spirit and it was good.

Shortly after, I learned that my mother had fallen after being transported to another sister, and she was in the hospital. It was a busy time for me and I was not able to get away. My mentally-challenged sister called me up and told me that while she was visiting my mother in the hospital, my mother looked around and said, "I can see! I can see!" It was God's stamp of approval on that very last blessed time with my mother.

I knew it was too much for my older sisters to care for a 99 year old woman, especially now that she broke her pelvis, so what would her quality of life be if she went back to either house? I was torn, and with deep, deep sorrow, I did not renew the contract. I prayed "Lord, You can take her, now. She'd be better off with you." Then I thanked God for letting me have her long enough to find out how much I loved her, and long enough to see how foolish I'd been to let such superficial things cloud my vision for so many years.

At the wake, I slipped a note under my mother's pillow that said, "Thank you for being my mother. I love you."

In the final analysis, it was really *my* vision that God restored.

"Don't You Trust Me"

I first met Jim at a prayer meeting where he was the guest speaker. After being married to a musician whose life was devoid of any spiritual values, it was a new experience to see a totally different type of man. I was impressed. I remember saying to the woman next to me, "Now there's a good man; if only I had met someone like him years ago."

The prayer group was formed by a handful of new believers. We had Sunday services at a private home, tried to organize, but it never developed into a regular church. During this period, through my piano business, I met Karen, a church organist. Our mutual love of God and of music drew us together, and I accepted her invitation to visit her church. It was exactly the spirit-filled congregation I had been looking for, so I not only joined, but ended up playing piano along with her. I didn't know when I went there that Jim was an elder in that church.

One icy day Jim was sent to my house by the pastor to pick me up when I was needed to play for a special program. After that, he showed up to drive me to church even when there was no ice and no special meeting. From then on, it seemed that every time I turned around I was tripping over Jim. My reluctance to become involved inspired a creative move by Jim to get my attention. He turned to my children, who desperately missed having a father, and won them over. In time, they were on one side of me pleading for a father and Jim was on the other side pleading for the children that he never had in his previous marriage. I really didn't want to marry and refused him twice. The pressure wore me down the third time, from both him and the children, and I finally consented. I was caught in the crossfire of other people's needs. It is never a good idea to do this.

It's hard to believe that I didn't notice anything out of the ordinary about Jim. It may have been the stars in my eyes as a new believer, seeing other believers as perfect human beings. Also, before you read the part in the Bible that talks about Wisdom, you see things in a naïve way. I thought that maybe Jim was God's way of sending me help to ease the strain of handling a household alone. Certainly God wanted my children to have a normal family life with a godly person at the head.

Why did I ignore my reluctance to marry? A new Christian is like a new baby, incapable of making sound decisions. Why didn't I question the Pastor who knew Jim for years and who refused to marry us? Instead of suspecting that the Pastor knew things about Jim that he wasn't at liberty to tell me, I attributed his refusal to his own reluctance to marry. He was a bachelor to the end.

My decision was sealed when Jim offered up the most beautiful prayer imaginable, thanking God for me and the children and promising God to be a good husband and father. I convinced myself that this was God's way to make up for my difficult life. I fully expected a normal, godly household, with happy, secure children.

To the religious world, Jim was a pillar of the church. He was actually a pillar of several churches. On Sunday morning and night, he went to an Assembly of God Church. On Monday night, it was the Episcopal Church. Tuesday night, he went to the Lutheran Church. Wednesday, the Assembly of God Church. Thursday, it was the men's non-denominational Gospel meeting. Friday, the Assembly of God Church, and Saturday morning it was the men's prayer breakfast. If anything was cancelled and he had a free night, he'd conduct his own prayer meeting, like the one where I first met him.

The good church people who saw Jim as a saint considered me the luckiest woman in the world to have caught his eye. Their positive input also influenced me. It never occurred to me that something is awry when one substitutes Church for Life. We always assume that church attendance is a measure of one's character. "Bad" people don't go to church, "Good" people do. I no longer believe this.

There must have been a reason why I backed down twice before marrying Jim. Something within me said no, but I thought it was my own fear. When the wedding ceremony turned out to be so spirit-filled, with my children beaming at the altar with us, I knew I had made the right decision. The church group gave us a wedding reception with their best home cooked dishes and heartiest blessings. The future held great promise for us.

Jim's dark side emerged almost immediately, beginning with the wedding. He complained of a headache. The complaining continued throughout the honeymoon. He griped about the cost of the hotel, the design of the room, the food, the other hotel residents, everything. What's worse, the honeymoon is supposed to be a romantic time, but he spent it talking about old girlfriends. I couldn't wait to get back home. If it weren't for the children and the church, I would have run for my life on my honeymoon and had the marriage annulled.

His attitude toward my children followed the same pattern, drastically changing after marriage. There was no connection between the beautiful prayer he lifted up and reality. The children looked to him with blind expectation and even took his name, but after a year of his erratic and harsh behavior, they resumed their own name and began praying to find their own father.

I don't know what movie Jim patterned family life after, but his idea of headship was power and control. Instead of a loving head of a household, Jim became the King and we were his subjects. He expected blind obedience. He was so legalistic and caustic that the children refused to go to church. When he proved to be insanely jealous, even accusing the elderly pastor of holding my hand a little too long during a handshake, I stopped going, also. None of us wanted to spend a minute more than necessary with him. Instead of unifying the family, he fractured it.

Jim's religious psychosis emerged in our first month of marriage. What he did was to go into a room alone, shut the door, and hand-wrestle the devil. The house shook with sounds reminiscent of a saloon brawl in an old Western movie. After awhile the door would slowly open and he'd emerge out-of-breath, sweating, and bruised, with his glasses hanging from one ear. The first time I witnessed it was the most shocking, and I trembled with fright as I heard violent sounds springing from the room. I had never seen anything like it. It was like something from The Exorcist.

After repeated episodes, I found the courage to confront him right after an episode.

"What's this all about, Jim?"

"That's between God and me!" he snapped, and stomped off angrily.

I didn't understand what it was, but I knew that whatever it was, it wasn't from God. It grieved me that I made such a terrible mistake and brought such insanity into my home. I tried to protect the children from it by turning on a noisy attic fan whenever Jim's demonic wrestling match occurred. I didn't learn for years that my son knew all along but said nothing.

On one occasion I burst into the room, pointed to his nose and shouted, "Jesus doesn't want you to do this!" He was sweaty, his hair was disheveled, and his forehead was bruised. He stopped, but only that time. It was useless for me to try to do anything. Jim's religious psychosis was too deep-seated for me to understand or to handle.

I was astonished at what I learned after seven years of marriage in a two-and-a-half-hour conversation with Jim's ex-mother-in-law who attended our church. She knew all about Jim and his religious psychosis. I was furious that she didn't have the wisdom or compassion to warn me.

"I didn't want to interfere," she answered.

"Interfere? You stood by and let me bring a madman into my house where you knew there would be children? Didn't you have any regard for their welfare?"

I also learned during that conversation that what he told me wasn't true. Her daughter did not divorce Jim "for religious reasons," she divorced him on the grounds of "extreme mental cruelty." This made my head spin.

Her final statement is forever burned on my soul: "If Jim didn't have the Lord, he'd be in a mental institution." And this was what I blindly stepped into.

Shortly after Jim and I married, I heard him tell a few of the church people, "Lucille doesn't think I do a good job at work." This puzzled me.

"Jim, I don't even know what a Systems Analyst does; how could I know whether you are doing a good job or not?" There were many of these misstatements, and I began to see that what went in his ears were scrambled by the time it came out of his mouth.

In marriage, Jim's low self-esteem resisted any compliment or encouragement. If I tried to build him up, he would bring about circumstances that would confirm his unworthiness. As hard as it was to raise a family on my own, that was nothing compared to trying to raise children with a psychopath in the house. The pressure of having his pathological thinking and behavior in the household brought constant chaos to our household.

He was so sure that he was on the verge of being fired from his job that after months of complaining, he submitted a letter of resignation. His superiors at work were so taken aback that they took him out to lunch and convinced him to stay. By this time, I was not surprised at his job misjudgment. I was only surprised that a person with his pathology could hold a job at all. Could he be an idiot savant who could operate on only one level? Was he different on the job? I never could figure it out.

Daily life with Jim brought endless confusion. His mind distorted everything. I got to a point where I could never believe or rely on anything he said because it was never true. Yet, he wasn't lying either. With his mental aberration, he perceived things differently. His mind constantly reversed things. Once, before Jim left on a business trip in October, he told me that John and Margie had gotten married that weekend. While he was gone, I learned that the couple wasn't getting married till November. When Jim returned, I said, "Jim, John and Margie are not getting married till November." He looked at me with indignation and said, "I know that! That's what I told you!"

After a few weeks, I asked "Jim, when did John and Margie marry?" He said "I *told* you they married in October!" A few weeks after that, if you asked him again, he would switch back to November. This showed the extent of his mental condition. It was hopeless. Nothing he said was accurate.

Life wasn't easy before Jim, but having him in our family removed even the little happiness we did have. Jim was suspicious of everyone and everything. He'd hide in the dark and eavesdrop; he was always accusing the children of stealing his money, money that he would subsequently find; he was extremely jealous of my son and even accused me of giving him bigger pieces of chicken at dinner; he expected to be obeyed instantly. Jim confused headship with domination and battered the three of us. He squelched all freedom and creativity. We couldn't even laugh without being accused of laughing *at* him. To my horror, I had brought a concentration camp existence into our household and my children and I were now prisoners. Had I picked a husband from the register of a mental institution, I could not have done worse.

I've never seen a parent complain when a young person did a chore without being asked, but with Jim, if you didn't have his permission—no matter what it was—he'd have a tantrum and make everybody miserable. Naturally, we went underground so we could breathe. There were parallel lives going on: when Jim was around and when he wasn't around.

While I had married this man to stabilize my family, we were more splintered than before. My children scattered and I was trying to protect my children and survive the emotional roller coaster that he brought.

Many times I wanted out, but Jim would appeal to my Christian beliefs. I went along with it for awhile, but eventually saw it as a calculated ploy.

"Don't you understand that I'm schizophrenic?" Holding my head, I'd say, "All right, let's find a therapist." The therapist gave Jim an assignment once, to list all the good and bad traits of his parents. Jim could not list one single good trait of either one, and could only list a few bad traits of his father. That spoke volumes to me. The sessions disintegrated, as did all other cures.

The next plea was "Don't you understand I have demons?" Then I'd say, "Well then, let's do something about it." He paid a large sum of money to an exorcist in Pennsylvania, returned renewed, and was "normal" for a time, then became seven times worse than before.

Then he excused his behavior by saying it was his health. Jim got a physical and was told that he had diabetes. When I found Jim eating a large piece of lemon meringue pie, I said, "Jim, should you be eating that?"

"Why not?"

"Because the doctor told you not to eat sweets or you could lose a leg."

"He never said that!"

So Jim would eat the sweets. That certainly may have contributed to his mood swings, anxiety, and truncated thinking, but my nerves were wearing thin. Life was unbearable for me, and my children avoided coming home.

Another doctor put Jim on a drug. Jim did not know what it was, so I looked it up and found that it was an anti-psychotic. In Jim's dark world, he couldn't comprehend why such a drug was prescribed to him. He considered himself normal.

It was very puzzling. No matter how wretched his emotional life was or how bizarre his behavior was, he was prospering financially. He was even recommended for weekend freelance work setting up whole bank systems. He was so accident prone that I couldn't believe he didn't break the computers that he had to deal with.

By the fifth year I could see that any effort to help Jim was a waste of time. I did my best to direct him to professionals but he never listened to them. He clung to his aberrations. It was all he knew. However, the stress of living with a dysfunctional person for so long and watching it drive my children away, was taking its toll on my health. I started to go downhill. By the seventh year, I was bedridden and had to physically remove myself to a connecting building to die in peace. I lay there and grieved for my children, wondering why God let me make such a terrible mistake.

Every once in awhile, Jim would call me up and say, "The Holy Spirit told me to apologize to you." These endless apologies were nothing more than new symptoms of old pathologies and were getting on my nerves. One day I said, "Jim, I forgive you for anything that you *have* done to me and my children, anything that you *are* doing to me and the children, and anything that you *will* do to us for the rest of your life, so there's no need to ever apologize again. YOU ARE FORGIVEN FOREVER! After awhile, he'd start up again with the phone calls and apologies, so one day I asked, wearily, "Jim, exactly *what* did the Holy Spirit tell you to apologize for?" Jim thought about that for a moment, then answered, "He didn't say." The whole exchange sounded like a Abbot and Costello pitch.

Thank God for Karen, the church organist who invited me to the little white church in the first place. She saw me going downhill and would call to pray with me. She was the perfect person to do this because not only were her prayers a soothing balm to my soul, but also she had the gift of prophesy. I couldn't see past the state that I was in. Death was hovering over me. Then Karen would say, "One day, you and your children will be sitting around the table happy, eating, talking, and laughing." My life was such a mess, so hopeless, that just *hearing* something positive was medicine to my bones. She said that I would be very wealthy in real estate. I wrote down most of her prophesies and still have them. This is what sustained me during this dark period.

I asked Karen to pray that Jim would leave, but that he would miraculously support the household until I regained my health and could work again. During very deep prayer, she said, "Thank you, God, that you are calling Jim to be your very own and that Lucille's children will be provided for." We fully expected that God was calling Jim out of my life to his own a ministry so that the children and I could heal and live a normal life.

One night Karen's prayers so invigorated me that I rose from my sickbed and stepped outside into the darkness in my nightgown. It was a balmy summer night and it was so pitch black out that the stars looked like beautiful sparkling diamonds in the sky. I would have loved to just raise my arms and disappear into the heavens. In my rare burst of joy, after Karen told me once again that I would be very wealthy, I said, "Karen, if it's true that God is going to prosper me, let's ask him to make it a million dollars." She took my flippant request seriously and prayed that God would bring me a million dollars.

At this time, I was subsisting on a daily cup of tea when I had the energy to make the long trek from the adjoining building to the main house. My body was so weak that I was a mere shell of my old self. It was 9:30am and Jim always left for work at 9:00, so by now he would be gone. Rising from my sick bed, I dragged myself wearily from the office building through the family room into the main house. To my utter consternation, he was there. I avoided looking into his eyes, which is what we are told to do when facing a mad dog.

I could feel his burning stare following me as I made a cup of tea. He tried to start an argument, then became even more enraged because I wouldn't feed into it. I didn't have an ounce of fight left in me. The weaker I became, the stronger he became.

I knew he was late for work and would have to cut short his attack. When he finally left, I locked the door behind him with relief and thanked God that he was gone. In a matter of seconds he was back at the door kicking and pounding. His fury and expletives resounded throughout the neighborhood. I unlocked the door with resignation and he exploded into the house screaming, "I forgot my briefcase and you locked the door! You locked the door!" I don't know why he was so upset about the locked door. He could have used the keys that were in his hand.

With each outburst, my stress threshold was just a little bit lower. On this day, there was no threshold left. His rage had sent me to the brink of collapse. My heart was palpitating and I broke into a cold sweat. This had gone on too long. If I didn't do something now, I may be dead and what would happen to my children? This man would never take care of them. I had to make one strong thrust to protect myself.

A call to my attorney assured me that with such extreme mental cruelty, I could be divorced in 90 days. Working on nervous energy, without even the cup of tea to sustain me, I sat at the typewriter and eight pages of charges flew from my fingers. Then I dressed slowly and painfully and got into my car.

Being back in my car was a semi-sweet experience after so long an absence. The wheel felt good under my frail fingers. For one brief moment, I recalled sitting at this very wheel, driving the children to school. Who would have thought that those hectic days would now be the good old days? Hectic was so much better than demonic.

Divorce was a rash decision to make with such poor health and no way to earn, but I couldn't handle one more day with Jim. And, too, what good would it be if I stayed till I died? Jim would take my house, fool another innocent Christian, remarry, and put my children in the street. If I didn't do something right now while I could still walk, the children wouldn't have a mother or a place to live. It would be better to lose financial security and try to keep my wounded family together, even if we had to go to a shelter.

It is almost impossible to describe my frame of mind as I headed towards the lawyer's office. Grief and exhaustion permeated every cell of my body and soul. I was too ill to cry. I was just stuck in an emotional numbness with no past and no future, only this overwhelmingly weary present.

I was about two miles from my house when the whirlwind in my head was suddenly interrupted. A soft but penetrating voice said, "Don't you trust me?"

It was so startling, I didn't know what to make of it. I had never experienced anything like this before. I pulled over and wondered what had just happened. I knew I was physically ill, but was I going mad, too? Had I caught Jim's delusions? I know that God often speaks through others and through events, but this is the first time I had ever heard an audible voice within myself.

The words resounded in my head over and over, "Don't you trust me?" What did it mean? What did God want from me? Didn't I have enough pain and suffering staying with a maniac for seven years? Was I not trusting God by going to a lawyer? Surely God didn't expect me to turn around and go back to my death bed.

I don't know how long I sat in the car with my arms on the steering wheel and my head on my arms. If nothing else, I needed to rest. It's so easy to serve God when things are going well, but not so easy when the life is draining out of you and your future looks bleak.

I had pulled off the road onto a small strip mall and sat in one of the parking spaces like a wounded bird, struggling to make sense out of life, but I didn't have the energy to think. There was a whirlpool in my head. The conflict was terrible. Everything within me didn't want to go back. I wanted him out of my life, out of my house, but God had spoken. If I wasn't going to trust Him when things were bad, *when* was I going to trust Him?

Despite the pull between my love of God and my love of my children, I knew that God had to come first. As the tears streamed down my face, I whispered the words of Job, "Though ye slay me, yet will I trust thee," and I turned around and returned to my sickbed, knowing fully that I was going to die. It was perhaps one of the hardest decisions I have ever had to make in my whole life, but what good would life be if I didn't obey God?

In exactly three months, the time it would have taken for my divorce to be final, Jim was dead. He was killed on his way home from his Thursday night Christian men's meeting by a drunk driver.

Because I chose to trust God's Voice and turned around, I was still Jim's legal wife and I received money from several insurance policies that I didn't know existed, and in time, from the negligence case. God had heard my silly and mindless prayer that one balmy night in my rare moment of pure joy during my illness and sent exactly what Karen prayed for . . . one million dollars.

The Broker

Scene I

After my husband died, I didn't know that he was insured through his work, and I was concerned about my bills. I was still very weak, so I was not able to work, yet. Some ladies were having a prayer meeting nearby, so I went to it. I felt I needed a group to help me petition God for help.

There were about five women around a kitchen table. As they asked each one what their prayer request was, I answered, "I need God to pay off my mortgage, as I am not able to work so I am concerned about keeping the house."

A woman piped up, the woman who was interested in Jim when he was free and chasing me, but she didn't know anything about my marriage with Jim. Only Karen knew, so this woman may have thought I had an idyllic married life, and there may have been a little competition there.

She said, "We can't pray for your mortgage. Mortgage is the same as rent, and I have to pay rent here."

They went on to pray for everything except my reason for being there, my mortgage. I remember how sad and dejected I felt on the way home. Does life ever let up, I wondered.

During the next month, an insurance check showed up unexpectedly from Jim's work for $200,000. With it, I paid off the mortgage and bought a two-family house. So now there was rental income. Karen said I would have real estate, and it was starting.

One Sunday the doorbell rang. I was still recuperating from Jim's death and all the health problems that I incurred from the marriage, so I was in my nightgown. I opened the door and standing there was the woman who refused to pray for my mortgage. She never said hello, but stood there like she was on a mission, and uttered five words, "Did your mortgage get paid?"

I looked that woman in the eye and said, "Of course."

She walked away without saying a word, and I never saw her again. I heard she moved out of state. I'm not sure I fully understood this incident, not even now. Was she hoping that my life would be a little harder than it already was or that God would not hear me because she couldn't have Jim? I don't know.

More money came in from Jim's personal insurance that he carried apart from work. Then in time, a large settlement came through from the wrongful death litigation.

Scene II

I have to laugh when I see the compelling ads on TV of the "caring" broker, a kindly father figure who will take care of all your financial needs. It was just that kind of broker that the Christian Lawyer brought me to that was dishonest. The lawyer was worried about the large sum I had and wanted to protect me. In his thoughtful ignorance, he put me right in the hands of a thief. The Christian Lawyer ultimately lost Four Hundred Thousand to this same man, so I know he had no part in the broker's stratagem. He was just dumb.

While the Broker told me there was no commission on the investments he put my money in, I later learned that he made Twenty Four Thousand Dollars off the top, on just this one investment. That was only the first of the many misstatements he made. This friendly paternal brokerage had trained all of their representatives throughout the country to spread the same falsehoods about the investments and within six years, there was a mammoth class action against them. The SEC ordered them to return over Three Hundred Million Dollars to investors. I did not take part in the class action since I had already begun a private action that I felt was led of God.

At the beginning, the broker, a man in his fifties, won my confidence, first with a recommendation by the Christian Lawyer, then by having a framed copy of the poem, "Footprints" on his wall. That's the one where Jesus is carrying us through our darkest hours, so there are only one set of prints. He also said that he was attending Bible studies. Nothing he said was true but merely a ploy to gain my confidence. There is a number you can call to check up on a Broker. Had I known this number at the start, I would have learned that he was fined a thousand dollars for lying on his application to become a broker. Why would he not lie to a client?

He answered my legal Complaint against him and the brokerage with so many lies that my head was spinning. He tried to exonerate himself by painting me as a sophisticated investor who knew what she was doing. Had I been a sophisticated investor, I would have seen through him.

Several weeks after he signed his name to the fraudulent statement, he dropped dead. His company did not tell me, another broker told me. This was shocking because he wasn't very old, and he didn't look sick at all. The brokerage thought I didn't know they lost their prime witness and tried to make it look like they had a strong case.

The lawyer that I had retained to handle this matter turned out to be as dishonest as the broker. He told me he had experience in Securities and he didn't. Every move he made was the wrong one and had to be corrected by the adversary. There was an arbitration clause in the agreement with the brokerage, yet my lawyer filed a lawsuit in a court of law. It had to be withdrawn, wasting time and money. We were working against a six year statute of limitations and there was only about five months left.

The brokerage advised my lawyer that the matter called for arbitration, so what does my lawyer do? He applies to an arbitration board – the wrong one. This, too, had to be withdrawn. Watching him was like watching a Charlie Chaplin movie, one bizarre move after another. Then one day he called me into his office and tried to persuade me to accept a Seventy Five Thousand Dollar settlement made by the broker. He said that it was a generous offer and that I should accept it. I remember ending that session with, "Whose side are you on, anyway?" I have often wondered what kind of offer the Brokerage made with this attorney for him to sell a client up the river.

In total frustration, I fired him and prayed about what to do next. Then I happened to see an article in a newspaper that said that the Securities and Exchange Commission went after a broker and got the people's money back. I thought, "Maybe that's what I should do, go to the SEC." I'd never heard of the SEC, but I felt led to write them. Why not? What could I lose?

I wrote my case up and sent it to the SEC with a copy to the Brokerage and within hours, the brokerage attorney called and wanted to see me. This came as a surprise since they were not this responsive when I had a lawyer.

People in finance told me that that I would never get all of my money back, that I would be lucky if I got 60% back. I never take seriously what people say, particularly experts. They rely on statistics, not miracles. I rely on a God who makes a way where there is none. The results? The brokerage returned the whole $340,000. They even had to pay interest because they did not return the money on time. I left the rest of the investments in blue chip stocks.

Several years later I ran into the man who made the decision to return my money and I asked him why he returned my full amount. I told him that people were telling me all over the place that you never get your full money back. He said, "That's true. But we saw that you were a writer, and we were having enough trouble as it was."

Once everything was over, I found it very distasteful to drive past my local crooked lawyer's office and see his name in big letters. And you couldn't avoid it since he was on a main road. I remember praying for his salvation, then saying, "Lord, can't you do something about that sign?"

Not too long after, a woman came right to my house and told me that my crooked lawyer was disbarred for helping himself to people's money. Needless to say, the sign came down.

The White Supremacist

W hen I moved from my home to the property that God gave me, I did not sell my house, I rented it out. Of the series of tenants that I had, one stands out. I should have rejected this family on the basis of their poor credit record, but I gave them a break. The man looked ill and they claimed that the bad credit report was due to high medical bills. I believed them.

There is a saying, "The Need is not always the Call." I saw their need from the start, but I did not pray about it and I took it upon myself to answer the call. It was a mistake.

I allowed their two dogs despite the fact that there was wall-to-wall carpeting throughout the huge colonial. They never mentioned the three cats, and soon after they moved in, they brought in a fourth cat which created havoc among the other cats. They all began marking their territory throughout the house.

These people were trouble from the start. In fact, their very first rent check bounced. They always made good on it eventually, but nothing was without complications and bank charges. The husband seemed bent on making trouble at every turn, and the wife spent her time trying to rectify the damage. He was like a wayward child who had to be kept in line by an apologetic wife.

In time, the wife revealed that her husband was a White Supremacist. He put up pictures of Hitler in the kitchen. The daughters could not bring classmates home because of this, and there was a lot of seething rage that burst into bitter family fights. The police records verify this.

While home all day with illness, the husband spent his time calling African-American organizations and broadcasts with insults and threats. He also made endless calls and threats to the Jewish man that his wife had had an affair with. What confused me was that the man was the son of Italian immigrants, his wife was Puerto Rican, and according to his Supremacists doctrines, they were all minorities, too. I didn't get it.

Since the man was home all day, he had the heat on 80 around the clock, so the heating bill was high. He blamed me for this, claiming that somehow something was connected to his furnace that was running up the bill. Even the utility company could not convince him that everything was proper and in order. To placate the man, I put a new thermostat in. Nonetheless, it was impossible to please this man. Once a complaint was satisfied, he'd find something else to complain about.

The cats urinated throughout the house and the odor was so bad, you could smell it from outside the front door. He insisted that it was a faulty sewer line and wanted me to redo the whole plumbing system, which would have cost thousands of dollars. He would not accept the fact that it was the cats. And so it went, each and every day, endless complaints, and there was no way to placate this man. There were something like 800 calls from him to my house in that year, and it was draining me. The low quality of their life was affecting the high quality of mine, and I was becoming depressed.

I didn't know that their marriage was shaky when they moved in, and with his constant rages, it was crumbling altogether. He never stopped reminding her that his father warned him about marrying a Puerto Rican, so she had to endure daily insults. If he stopped there, she could have tolerated it, but he went on to call her very bad names because of her affair, all of this in front of the children. When she decided to get a divorce, he wasn't budging. He said that he was going to stay in the house, not pay the rent, and it would take the landlady—me—a year to get him out because of his illness.

When I heard this, I could hardly bear the thought of dealing with this demonic man. I remember going to church with a heavy burden on my heart. The pastor announced from the pulpit, "Is there anyone who needs prayer? Please step into the aisle, and someone please pray for them." I stepped into the aisle.

I was so overburdened, I couldn't even look up. A woman's voice asked me what I needed prayer for, and all I could say was, "Bad tenant." The voice said,

"I've been through this so I know what you're going through," and she prayed a beautiful prayer that God would get this man out of my house and my life. This simple, spirit-filled prayer was all I had to cling to, and I hung on for dear life.

The next day I got a call from the wife. She said, "My husband was taken away last night." I was shocked.

"What do you mean?" I gasped.

She told me what happened and it was clearly the Hand of God.

"My youngest daughter came home at 1:00 AM and this infuriated my husband. He went crazy and was screaming and yelling and about to beat us. He did not see me dial 9-1-1 on my cell phone, and I left the phone open on the table. The dispatcher heard his insane ranting and sent the Psycho Squad, a special branch of police, and they took him to a mental institution."

It was over.

The Poison Case

Scene I

It was a cold January day when there was a high incidence of influenza and I was one of the unlucky ones. I couldn't shake it. I was ill on and off for two months. The end of February, it had traveled from my chest to my throat. My fever didn't break to low grade till early March, even though my ear was infected. While I felt a little better, my appetite was still poor and I was very weak. It was at this time that Ethel called.

Ethel missed me. We were friends for a long time, but the past year we had been getting together every week to explore new and different restaurants. My illness had interrupted what had became our weekly foray, and she wasn't going to stand for it any longer. It was now the first Friday in March, and she called me up.

"It's time to explore a new restaurant, Lucille."

"I really don't feel up to it."

"Well, you're not going to get stronger lying in bed."

"Ethel, I really have no appetite and I can't taste or smell anything."

"That's all the more reason we should go to our favorite restaurant. You'll gain an appetite the minute you see the delicious sole franchaise in front of you."

Our conversation went on like this for awhile. I don't know if it was the cabin fever I was beginning to feel from being indoors so long, or the fact that my fever had broken and I felt a little better, I told her I would dress warmly and pick her up.

Scene II

I remember the exact time we entered the restaurant, a little past three, because we asked the hostess if we were too late for lunch. The place was virtually empty with maybe one or two couples in the whole glass and brass setting. We ordered the sole franchaise and they brought a salad first. The instant the vinegar in the salad touched my throat, it set off a coughing jag the likes of which I had never experienced in my whole life. It was so bad, I had to rush to the ladies room on the brink of vomiting. I saw my face in the mirror when I lifted my head up from the sink, and it was crimson with beads of perspiration dripping down. The retching was so loud, it must have been heard all over this empty restaurant, as the waitress came in to see if I was alright.

It finally passed and I returned to our table where the food had already come. The tea felt good on my throat, but I had a difficult time eating. Without a sense of taste or smell, I had to go by texture. The mashed potatoes were smooth and went down easily, but the fish took a while. With Ethel's goading that I needed to regain my strength by eating, I managed to down around half the meal.

I didn't notice right away that Ethel took one bite then quit. In the past, she didn't always finish her meal so she could bring half of it to her son, so I didn't question it. I was starting to not feel well again, and just wanted to get out of there. When I brought Ethel home, she quickly dropped down on one couch and I on the other and I realized that she hadn't taken any food home for her son. When I asked Ethel why she didn't eat her meal, after all, it was her idea to go there, she said, "The fish didn't taste right. I should have sent it back."

"And you let *me* eat it? You knew I couldn't taste or smell, and you let me eat bad fish?"

Scene III

On my drive home, there was a news bulletin about an epidemic of stomach virus. By the time I got home, I went straight to bed. By Saturday evening, I began getting stomach cramps followed by vomiting and diarrhea. I thought, Oh no, I've caught the stomach virus. I should never have gone out in my weakened condition. The news said it would last forty-eight hours, but by Monday, I was not better,

I was worse. I had no sleep over the weekend, and now the vomiting was projectile. I wondered where everything was coming from, as I hadn't eaten in a week except for the little bit I ate in the restaurant. Certainly, that was gone the very first time I vomited. I felt I was vomiting up my own body.

Monday was no better, so I went to the emergency room where they did tests and said they would call me. I had my phone turned off so I could rest, so they reached me on Wednesday with, "You tested positive for Salmonella.."

I didn't really know what salmonella was, but I recalled hearing or reading about outbreaks on cruise ships or cookouts. I never thought I would ever contract such a thing.

She continued, "Have your doctor admit you to the hospital immediately."

I had no doctor, so she gave me the names of two, and I chose the closest one. I called him and reported the test findings, and when I got there, he took one look at me and told me to go straight to the hospital. By this time, my pressure had dropped to 88 over 66. I felt like I was dying.

The doctor had called the hospital, so they were expecting me, and rushed me through. The next thing I knew, I was hooked up to an IV with all sorts of solutions entering my veins. I later learned that nothing can be done for salmonella except pump a high dose of antibiotics in you. According to the nurse's report, I had diarrhea every fifteen minutes around the clock for several days. Eventually, my system got quiet and I was able to rest. After a total of eight days, I was able to go home, but it wasn't over. I had cramps and diarrhea everyday when I tried to eat, and fevers would come and go for at least a year. I had to retire, as the pain and diarrhea would strike unexpectedly, so I had to stay close to home.

The doctor put me on a medicine whose side effect was constipation, and that seemed to help offset the diarrhea. The trouble is, you couldn't eat for two hours before or after you took the medicine, so it was hard to find the right time. And if I forgot to take it, I would be doubled over in the pain if I ate. I wondered if this was to be a permanent state. Three separate people in the country prayed with me weekly, so there was a lot of prayer for me.

Scene IV

After a year or so, I was asked by my son to testify for his friend, who was abandoned by his parents and was getting into trouble. After my testimony, the judge was lenient with him, but I never saw the boy again. At that hearing, the lawyer and I had a conversation and I told him all about the salmonella attack. Though he did not think it was a good case, he took it on contingency, anyway. We didn't go to court for three years, and all this time, my prayer partners in California, Connecticut, and North Carolina continued to pray with me. The amazing thing was that all three – who did not know each other – all said the same thing, that the case would go to court and that it would turn out much better than anyone would expect.

It was very difficult holding onto these words with a lawyer's constant negative input. George spent the whole three years telling me that it was not a good case, that our state did not hand out good medical settlements. I remember his saying, "Now if this was Texas, you'd be a millionaire," and so it went. Month after month he'd call me up or call me to his office and try to have me sign off on the case. He even showed me data that conclusively proved that there are little or no medical settlements in our state, so the whole case was a waste of time. I got to a point where I was teetering on the line between what my prayer partners were saying and what George was saying. I was torn; after all, wasn't this lawyer the expert? And I knew that he wasn't lying; he was simply going by the facts before him. But then, God is the ultimate expert. Even with such legal provocation, I was compelled to choose God.

His pressure to drop the case was bordering harassment, so what I did was to make a copy of the law that said that the lawyer cannot make a decision for the client, and I faxed it to George. He didn't bother me after that. . .until we got to court.

Scene V

That day in October, we all met at the courthouse; George, the opposing attorney, and me. Both of them came down on me like I was the enemy. Neither one wanted to pick a jury and go to trial. They were both holding back. I remember the other lawyer saying, "Even if you should win—and I doubt that you will—

we will Appeal, so you will spend whatever you may win on further litigation." That was a pretty convincing argument and it took everything I had to focus on God, not them. It wasn't as if my health was good. I was still on morning medication, so I didn't have breakfast. My days all began in a weakened state, and it would have been so easy to simply settle, but I felt it would be showing lack of faith. I was being pummeled into the ground by two determined and energetic lawyers, but I had to put God first. He spoke and I had to listen.

Next, they went into the judge's chambers and were in there a very long time. When they came out, they said, "The judge wants to speak to you." I thought, Here it comes. And sure enough, the judge did everything to encourage me to settle short of ordering me. He said, "The last medical case that came in, the client wanted $85,000. Do you know what he left with? $12,000. As he spoke, I felt my body getting weaker and weaker, and I prayed to myself, "God, you're going to have to help me. These legal giants are wearing me down."

When I stepped out of the judge's chambers, the two lawyers greeted me with great anticipation, expecting that the judge would have more success with me than they, but I said only one thing, "George, pick a jury." The lawyers were like two balloons deflating, and George would not speak to me after that. It is not easy to follow what God wants you to do in the face of such ominous opposition. However, in defense of George, I will say that once he realized that he was going to have to go through with a trial, he switched gears, and became the powerful lawyer that I knew he was.

Scene VI

With the judge on the bench, the jury in their box, and my lawyer and I at one table and the opposition lawyer at another table, the judge launched the case with a few introductory words. George stood up and said. "Your Honor, I want to put on record that I did everything I could to have my client settle, but she wouldn't do it. She even sent me the law that said it was her decision to make." I know why he did this. He did this to protect himself from any liability that might occur when we lose the case and I come away with nothing. That's what he was thinking.

There ensued two full days of trial that included two opposing Microbiologists and a string of wit-nesses for both sides. As beautiful as this restaurant was, they were not as sanitary as they should have been, nor did they refrigerate their eggs, a source of salmonella. And when the owner testified, she was inaccurate. She said that the Health Department inspects her restaurant every six months, but the records showed that there was no inspection for over a year, and at the last inspection, there were viola-tions which were not corrected.

Ethel testified. She knew me before the poisoning and knew me after and was able to witness to the change in my life. Needless to say, we did not explore new restaurants any longer and for a time, I had misgivings against Ethel because she sat there and let me eat the food that she knew was bad. While we had gone to same restaurant, and ordered the same dish, I was the one who became dangerously ill. It was because she was in good health and barely tasted it, and I, feverish and without a sense of taste, ate a bigger portion of it. She was in good health and had slight aftereffects for only one day after eating the fish. I, on the other hand, had been sick for a few months prior to this, and I was not fully recuperated when we went out to eat, so my resistance was low, plus I ate a lot more of the fish than she. I eventually forgave Ethel. She didn't do it deliberately, but I still don't know why she let me eat that bad food.

Scene VII

When the jury was out, George and I sat in a conference room, and I watched him spiral downward. He was disturbed and irrational.

"I don't know why I took this case. I knew it wouldn't go anywhere. Do you know what this case is worth? Do you know? Well, you're lucky if you see Thirty Thousand before paying for the expert witness and expenses, and a third to me. That's if you get anything at all."

Then he added, "When you lose everything, don't come crying to me."

I remember saying, "George, you're the only one crying."

That didn't stop him. I had to listen to a few hours of his negative soliloquy, which was worse than the stress of the whole case.

Finally, we were summoned back into the court-room. The jury had a verdict.

The judge asked the foreman to stand, and he did. The judge asked what the verdict was on the restaurant, and he said, "Guilty."

The judge asked what the damages were, and he said, "One Hundred Fifty Thousand Dollars."

The judge was so taken aback at this verdict, that he asked if the jury had any questions, that he would answer them in his chambers. The foreman answered, "No."

Again, he repeated that he would gladly take them into his chambers and discuss any questions they may have, and the jury declined.

Then the judge proceeded to add another Forty thousand for medicine, and he tacked on interest retroactive to the day the case was filed, none of this to be shared with the lawyer. I remember the figure, because it was the same as the boiling point: Two Hundred and Twelve Thousand Dollars.

George stood up stiffly and said, "I want to put it on record that sometimes the client is right." With that, the trial was over.

George didn't know what to say to me, but I knew what to say to him. "You know, George, the only obstacle in this case was you." He didn't care what I said. There were a bunch of lawyers lined up to congratulate him. I didn't even know they were in the room listening, but I guess lawyers watch each other. They were curious because of how badly medical cases went, and everyone was shocked.

On our way out of the courthouse, George walked like he was floating on air, and boasted, "That was an easy Fifty Thousand." Maybe for him, it was, but dealing with him made it a nightmare.

It is almost impossible to hold fast to God's Word with so much pressure from the so-called experts. You find yourself abandoned by everyone around you because they think you're crazy. It takes every ounce of faith to ignore what you see with your eyes and hear with your ears to hold fast to what you know God wants you to do.

I later learned that it was the judge who estimated the case to be Thirty Thousand, and he didn't want to be wrong, which is why he invited the jury to go to his chambers and discuss any questions they may have. They did not know that in worldly thinking, they were right. The judge was right, as well as both lawyers, and it would have turned out their way under natural condition, but God was in it.

Ultimately, the supernatural always circumvents the natural.

The Stroke

The stroke happened the evening of August 11, 2009. It came less than two weeks after my gall bladder removal, so the doctor and I suspect that there may have been a connection.

The first symptom occurred when I was sitting at my desk late one night reading something on the computer. My right hand moved on its own. I jumped. I couldn't understand why I was not in control of my hand, or rather, how my hand gained control of itself. It was as though a foreign object moved toward me that made me flinch.

I inspected both hands and noticed that they were not the same color. My left hand was pink and my right had a grey pall. I didn't know what to make of it. I went to bed somewhat perturbed. My right hand continued to annoy me, and I remember removing it from sight by burying it under the covers. If it was no longer part of my body, I didn't want to look at it.

The next day I had many errands to do, and in the morning, I stopped by to drop something off at Ruth's house. She was not at home, so I called her on my cell phone and left a message. In the afternoon Ruth called me back, but I was out, so we did not make contact that day. Our practice was to make calls during the day while her husband was at work. But this day, because we kept missing each other all day, we made an exception. It would be alright since my message to her would be brief.

I called her at 7:30pm and I barely got a sentence out when my words became garbled. Ruth shouted, "Hang up! You're having a stroke!" I'm not sure I even believed her, because other than the strange speech, I felt fine.

The next thing I knew, the police were at the door. It's a good thing that Ruth called them because by this time, it wasn't just garbled words. I couldn't speak at all. The ambulance was right behind them and I was rushed to the hospital. The police called Ruth back and thanked her for calling so quickly. They said, "You saved your friend's life." After this, Ruth called her prayer group and they had a prayer vigil for me.

Only a week earlier I had given Ruth my son's telephone number. It never occurred to me in the prior ten years to do this, but for some reason, I gave it to her at this time. If she didn't have his number, things would have turned out differently.

She called my son, and he got to the hospital before the ambulance. He lives quite a distance away, so even that was unbelievable. While I was having tests, the hospital contacted a neurosurgeon and he was on his way in. It was urgent that a family member be there to choose a plan of action. The

CAT scan showed a clot on the left brain, the area that deals with speech. The neurosurgeon gave my son three options: 1) Do nothing and let the clot try to work itself out; 2) administer a drug that would break up the clot, but it can cause hemorrhaging; 3) Go in there and remove the clot.

My son chose the third, and it turned out to be the best one in my case. He told me later that as they wheeled me into the operating room, the right side of my face was already dropping. It was the same when they wheeled me out three hours later. I don't remember anything but the mask they quickly slapped over my face when they rushed me into the operating room. Next thing I knew, I was in Intensive Care.

The following morning, my son returned to the hospital with great trepidation. He didn't know what to expect. As he entered my room, he said a wary, "Hi, Mom." When I answered an energetic, "Hi, Son," he almost fell back out the door. My face was normal, my speech returned, and it was as though the stroke never happened.

The neurosurgeon came by to see me. He held up fingers and asked, "How many?" I answered, "Don't you know how to count?" He smiled from ear to ear when he heard me speak so clearly. It meant that the procedure was successful. Word must have gotten around because after that, just about every doctor in the hospital came by to see me. One by one, they marched in and held up fingers for me to count. I was starting to wonder if part of their job description was that they not be able to count. But they were all stopping by to see the miracle for themselves. Apparently, not too many people come out of a stroke unaffected.

I didn't comprehend the dangers, not only of the stroke itself, but of the procedure. To get to my left brain where the clot was lodged, the doctor had to go in through my right groin, up the main artery in my torso, up through my neck vein to the left brain. I had no idea that I went through such a lengthy and sensitive procedure. You would think that there would be a little discomfort after such an intricate and delicate procedure, but there wasn't. I felt normal and ready to go home immediately, but they needed to keep me there for observation for a few days.

I knew that something out-of-the-ordinary had taken place when I heard the nurses refer to me as the "miracle lady." One nurse also said to me, "What are you doing here in Intensive Care? This place is for sick people," and they moved me to another floor. It was rare to see someone come through such an ordeal without one single aftereffect.

When you're ready to leave the hospital, a nurse routinely checks you for home care. When she examined me, she said, "Nah, you don't need home care." Even the physical therapist that took me for a walk through the halls and had me climb up and down stairs said, "Nah, you don't need therapy." I didn't need anything except to get home and have a good meal.

In assessing the whole experience, I can see that my total recovery was due to a series of miracles that were so perfect, it *had* to be orchestrated by

God from beginning to end: giving my son's number to Ruth the week before; our rare evening call just as the stroke was happening—how would I know I couldn't speak since I was alone and do not walk around talking to myself; Ruth recognizing immediately that it was a stroke and taking such fast action; my son's right choice to the doctor; and most importantly, the prayer vigil that protected me the whole time.

The Promised Land

Chapter I

The Little White Church Revisited

Turning The Pulpit Over

There was a faint stirring in my heart to visit the quaint white country-like church where my late husband had been elder, and where I had enjoyed many memorable experiences.

In my three-year absence, major changes had occurred in the church. The elderly Pastor, who was loved and respected by all, had retired after many years of unblemished service. He had sensed for a long time that with the influx of young families to the church, an old bachelor pastor like himself was not a suitable role model. With great humility, he turned the pulpit over to his youth pastor, who was married and the father of two small children, a picture-perfect leadership. As always, the kindly old pastor had the interest of his congregation at heart.

Revisiting

I felt a slight trepidation the Sunday I pulled into the church parking lot after so long an absence. I arrived early and could feel the memories of the past welling up in me as I slipped through the ground floor side door. I wondered how many times I had ascended these stairs to the foyer in the ten years I attended this Little White Church.

Entering the sanctuary was like stepping back in time. I sat in my old pew, center left, and looked around. Nothing had changed. It was the same bare windows and walls, the same bland industrial carpeting, the same worn oak pews, the same unadorned altar—more like a stage. But somehow it felt different, like visiting the old familiar neighborhood where strangers now lived in your old house. Sitting there alone in the church, I thought about my close friend and prayer partner, Karen, whom I met thirteen years earlier.

The Healing

Karen was the one who invited me to this church in the first place to hear a guest speaker named George Otis, a charismatic evangelist with a brilliant delivery and a message that kept you spellbound. At the end, he said, "Those who want healing, go through the door on the right. And those who want the Baptism of the Holy Spirit, go through the other door, on the left." I went through the healing door.

I'm not sure what I believed at the time. All I know is that my doctor would feel the swollen nodule on my thyroid and say, "You'd better get that thing out." I remember telling him, "You'll have to catch me first." With two children to support and no medical, plus no savings to speak of, there was no way I could go for an operation. This healing call was *it* for me.

The Healing line was fairly long, so when Mr. Otis got to me, I kept it brief. When he asked, "What seems to be the problem?" I pointed to my neck and answered, "Thyroid."

With this, he lunged at my neck, cast the lump out in the Name of Jesus, and sent it to the deepest sea. This deliverance was so loud and unexpected, there is no doubt in my mind that anything that didn't belong in my neck would have no choice but to jump out to avoid another bombastic shout. Strangely enough, all my tests from then on, up to the present, registered normal.

After this, I began attending Karen's church. She played organ on the right side of the altar, and after attending awhile, I played piano across from her, on the left. Because the old pastor was a high energy person who loved to sing, the music was upbeat and lively. I remember the beautiful worship, the miracles, and the answered prayers. It was a blessed time.

Karen

Karen was spiritually gifted. When we prayed, her faith transported us to the very throne of God. Never before had I experienced such a deep level of spirituality where you are no longer in the physical realm, but become pure spirit. At this level, she would prophesy things to come in my life. Her positive prophesies were what I needed to hear at the time. I was a single parent with total support of two children, a mortgaged house, struggling to make ends meet. Having no family or friends in the area to help, and nowhere to turn, I often felt like I was on a flimsy raft in the middle of the ocean during a storm . . . always one step away from drowning. I needed *something* to get through life, and her prayers and prophesies were that something. They refreshed my soul and gave me something positive to look forward to in my difficult, and at times hopeless, situation.

A few years later, Karen was my Matron of Honor when I married an elder in that church. She and her husband were by my side seven years after that when my husband was killed by a drunk driver. The month before his death, Karen prophesied that God would take him to be His own, but for some reason, we did not interpret it as death. We assumed that God would open up a special ministry for him. In looking back, it was obvious what it meant, but neither one of us realized it.

Death Premonitions
She was not the only one to predict my husband's death. Early that year, my husband, himself, had an ominous foreboding and said "I don't think I'm going to live very long." This startled me, as he was only 48 and had no life-threatening disorder. I couldn't imagine why he would say this.

There were other strange occurrences. Four people that year told me that I would be a widow, including my own mother, who told a relative that she didn't think my husband would be around toward the end of the year. These were people who never met my husband, so I found it odd that they would say this, but I didn't take it very seriously.

My husband always claimed that he never dreamed but just before the accident, he had a dream that was so vivid, it woke him up and he wrote it down on a piece of junk mail. I still have it. He dreamed that he was driving along a road, entered a curve and crashed into a rock. It was an eerie preview of what was to come. One night, after a men's religious meeting, he was driving home and entered a curve. Just as he entered it, a drunk driver entered the curve from the opposite direction. His pick-up never made the curve, but plowed right into the driver's side of my husband's car. The impact was so great, my husband ended up in the back seat. As in the dream, he entered a curve and crashed into a rock, only the rock was a speeding pick-up.

Karen's Prophesies

Karen prayed with me often. Prior to my husband's death, she continued to tell me that I would have money and own valuable real estate. I was in such poor health I didn't expect to live, much less have wealth, but it was good to hear, even if I didn't believe it.

One summer night, I was in a very nostalgic mood when Karen called. I got up out of my sickbed and stepped through the sliding door to a chaise lounge. I wanted to pray under the stars. It was such a clear night, I felt you could reach up and touch a star. She mentioned the wealth, again, and I said, "If God wants to give me a lot of money, why not ask Him to make it a million." It was a flippant remark, in keeping with my strange mood, but she took me seriously and prayed for the million. I will never forget that night. I even remember what I was wearing, a pink cotton nightgown.

It was at my husband's wake that a group from the Little White Church came to pay their respects, and Karen pointed to one of them and said, "You will inherit that property within two years." I remember turning my head toward her and saying, mindlessly, "Why?" I was already overwhelmed to be at my husband's wake, and I couldn't bear the thought of more people dying. I discounted the thought.

At the time of my husband's death, we had been living four years in a house we bought from the widow of a doctor. It was a 2-storey, 4-bedroom Colonial, with a large attached recreation room that led to a medical building where the doctor had his general practice for many years. After my husband's death, there was no way I could live in two buildings, so I rented out the main 4-bedroom house and lived in the medical building myself. It was perfect for me; like a small ranch house.

Insurance money came through on a double indemnity accident policy through his company that I didn't know existed. I paid off the mortgage and bought a two-family building for income. Karen's prophesies had begun to unfold, but by this time, she had moved far away, and we lost touch. It was as though she was put in my life for a season, but now her time was up. My children were grown and I was alone. The church was a familiar place where I felt safe. When I decided to visit the Little White Church, I think I was reaching into the past for a future. I never dreamed that this innocent move would be so far-reaching.

The New Pastor

Sitting in the pew, my reverie was abruptly interrupted as people entered the sanctuary and began filling the pews around me. I didn't recognize anyone, with the exception of perhaps four people, two of them were my friend Mary's children. I expected to see more familiar faces but the members that I knew in the past had persuaded the old retired bachelor pastor to start his own little church and they all migrated there. In only a three-year absence, I was now a visiting stranger in the Little White Church that had, at one time, been my home away from home.

The old pastor was always up at the pulpit singing joyously as people entered, but whoever this new pastor was, he was conspicuously absent. I wondered where he was, or if there was a pastor at all. When everyone was seated and the clock reached the appointed time, there was a booming fanfare, the kind that announces the arrival of royalty. It was a cue for the pastor and his wife, who were now standing at the back of the sanctuary, to join hands and strut majestically down the aisle. He deposited her at the front pew and took his place at the pulpit.

Their pompous entry didn't sit well with me. I hadn't seen anything like this since a documentary of the coronation of Queen Elizabeth. I struggled with myself to reserve judgment and nearly succeeded until I heard the sermon. He said something about God's writing on his forehead, as though he were the Chosen One. Again, I fought to suppress judgment. Despite these misgivings, I continued to attend. My roots were anchored in this church.

As time went on, more questions arose in my mind about this pastor. A young couple I knew was planning to marry. Because they respected me, they decided to go to the pastor of the church I was attending. I didn't feel good about it, but I said nothing to them. I wouldn't allow myself to speak against the pastor.

They had an interview with him, then called me up. They said he was way out-of-line, that he asked inappropriate questions, especially about sex, which was embarrassing and humiliating. They never went back and were married elsewhere. I was relieved, but their experience added more questions in my mind about this pastor.

The Chief Elder

One Sunday in church, I had an earache. Expecting to have the same experience I had with George Otis, the evangelist who prayed for my thyroid, I decided to go up to the altar for prayer after the service. People were lined up in front of the Elders, and I just stepped randomly into one of the lines. It turned out to be the Chief Elder, right hand man of the pastor. Immediately after his prayer, my ear went deaf. That should have warned me something was amiss, but again, I reserved judgment. I didn't know at the time that this Chief Elder was being groomed by the Pastor to be a Faith Healer. My worsened earache aroused my suspicions since the Chief Elder did not seem to have that Gift, but again, I tried not to judge. In fact, once I learned that he was a building contractor, I asked his opinion on a technical building matter as a way of becoming acquainted with him and becoming closer to the church. It was a question about whether two different roof levels could ever be joined.

I wrote in my prayer book that I had the feeling – a very strong feeling – that this Chief Elder would be an important part of my life. It never entered my mind that a person could be a part of your life in a negative sense. Whenever he was around, I suppressed an unexplainable wariness that kept rising up, but told myself that he had to have superior qualities for a pastor to choose him above all other elders to be his right-hand man and share power with him. I had a lot to learn.

When I asked the Chief Elder the roof question, he asked for my survey. In looking back, I can see that there was no reason to look at the survey to answer a technical question. I was so naïve, believing the best of anyone connected with a church, and realize, now, that he was just nosey. Being so open and honest, I didn't question his reason and simply complied. He wrote back that he couldn't help me. What did that mean? I didn't ask him to *do* anything, just to answer a question, so I called him up. We clashed like brass symbols. He wasn't the least bit interested in answering my question—maybe he didn't know the answer—he was only interested in knowing about my property. He asked over and over whether I was renting out the main house, which puzzled me. What was so important about that? I saw no relevance between my roof question and what I was doing with the house.

I asked point blank why that was so important to him. He spoke like a town official and told me that it was illegal to live in the medical building and rent out the house. I remember saying, "How can I physically live on a double property that has two separate houses, two separate driveways, separate utilities, separate yards, and separate house numbers? And how can I pay taxes on this double property?"

"Get a loan!!" he barked.

Was this man serious? Why would anyone expect a person, particularly a widow, to borrow to pay taxes on a four bedroom empty house? It was the most absurd advice, neither godly nor practical. I could sense that this man was fiercely fighting to control me. His blunt attitude and demanding suggestions had very little to do with renting, but was somehow more involved with control. This was a far cry from the loving church it had been under the old singing pastor.

If the Chief Elder had stopped there, I would not have lost total respect for him, but when he saw that he could not badger me into submission and that I wouldn't buckle to his power, he tried to intimidate me.

"Do you know what you have?" he ranted. "You have a Demon of Renting."

"A what? What on earth are you talking about?"

I knew beyond a doubt, now, that there was something not right about this man. All I asked was a theoretical question about two roof levels, and he used it as a means to attack my life. He was devoid of love or compassion and, in my eyes, did not believe in either God, or the church. He was not even as kind as some unbelievers. He was rude, harsh, tyrannical and controlling. It was obvious that he exploited his position as Chief Elder to badger people into submission. He thoroughly relished the power he was given over the congregation, and he expected to be obeyed without question. Since he could not get that obedience from me, he attacked me from every direction. I do not believe in controlling others, nor expect others to control me. No, we were not going to be friends. In fact, judging from his attitude, it looked like we were going to be enemies.

The Inspection

A few days later, there was pounding on my rec room door. It was the Building Inspector. He said he was responding to a complaint. I found this odd in light of the recent disagreement with the Chief Elder. I didn't want to believe that a church official would be so vindictive as to use spite to get the upper hand. You don't expect a "payback" mentality from a church official; maybe a politician, but never an

Elder. Why were my living arrangements so important to him in the first place? What was it to him?

The Building Inspector entered through the recreation room entry and said, "Wasn't this door a window?" I told him the truth, that it was a long window that had been extended one foot down to make it a door. He inspected it and said, "You have a steel header; it's secure." Then he added, "Good job," and he moved on.

He walked through the rec room to the connecting door to the house, and I introduced him to my tenant. He was polite and courteous, and sat at the tenant's table and had a cup of coffee. Still thinking about the rec room entry, I asked him if I need a permit for that, and he said, "That depends on how good the coffee is." I guess the coffee was very good, because I did not hear from him again; and he did not say one word about my renting the house and living in the medical side.

My Letter To The Pastor

Concluding that if a Chief Elder is so determined make trouble for a church member, perhaps he is also deceiving the pastor, too, so I wrote a letter to the pastor explaining the whole situation to him. I told him that the Building Inspector behaved the way I expected the Chief Elder to behave, and the Chief Elder behaved the way I expected a Building Inspector to behave. The pastor's startling response was "Take your un-forgiveness to the Cross." This wasn't a typical response from a Pastor. A normal response would be to look into the matter by calling a meeting between all parties to resolve the matter.

Months later, the church secretary revealed that the pastor had read my letter to the Chief Elder, and they had a good laugh together. They were in cahoots, a real Demonic Duo. And she also revealed that this pastor dismissed *every* church complaint with the same advice, "Take your un-forgiveness to the Cross." It was hard to believe that this was the same church that I had attended in the past. Something was dreadfully wrong. I should have just left, but I was glued to the situation much like getting caught up in a mystery novel and wanting to see how it all turned out.

The Chief Elder's Lie

The Chief Elder, in retaliation for my letter to the pastor, began circulating a rumor that I didn't like him because I had asked him to do illegal construction and he refused. My friend Mary and her husband heard about this rumor from their children, who still attended this church. They were incensed at such an atrocious lie and confronted the Chief Elder about it, but talking to a man with so little honesty or integrity was a waste of breath. He just scoffed at them. It was as though this Chief Elder had such disrespect for people, he treated them like imbeciles, smiling throughout his sarcastic disdain, much like a cat that plays happily with a mouse while killing it.

In the middle of all this confusion, I ran into a member of the church who had been attending since the old singing Pastor days. He was fairly young and

I remember his wedding, and then the birth of his child. He did not leave with the old pastor as did most of the older members, but he told me that he was taking his family out of this present church. I asked why, and he said that there's no more teaching there, and the Pastor has changed some of the by-laws. "Many people are leaving," were his final words. That was the last time I saw him.

I agreed with what he said, and maybe I should have left, too. Nothing looked good there, but still, I stayed. I think I just wanted to see how things turned out. Even in a class B movie, bad as they are, you still want to see how it ends. Do the natives finally kill the monster? Maybe I hung on just to find out.

The Chief Elder Sublets to Church Group

It wasn't long before I learned that the Chief Elder had sublet a room in his office suite to a small group from the church. In other words, he was doing exactly what he was accusing me of doing: renting out part of a whole to help defray expenses. He seemed to think that if others did it, it was demonic, but if *he* did it, it was all right. However, sublet-ting to church members was either a sign of gross arrogance or unbridled stupidity, because it proved to be his undoing. By putting godly people right in the office where he conducted shoddy business, he was flaunting his unsavory business practices. They heard him using foul language; lying to people; taking deposits and not doing the work; he cleverly gave his young secretary the legal right to sign his checks which later almost got her jailed. He was a perfect candidate for the "Shame On You!" TV program, where dishonest business people were exposed on camera.

Occasionally, the police would pick him up at the office on a victim's complaint, but he was unruffled by it all. In fact, he was amused at his rattled church brethren as police led him out. It also became known that his son was running away from home periodically, occasionally showing up at my friend Mary's house for a place to sleep. In other words, while this Chief Elder was going about telling others how to conduct their lives, his own business and family life were in shambles. I knew that there was something unsavory about this Chief Elder, but I never imagined the extent of it.

The small church group, in accordance with the Scriptures, counseled the Chief Elder again and again, admonishing him to mend his ways. They told him that he cannot be godly on Sunday and dishonest the rest of the week, but they got nowhere with him. Rules were for other people, not for him, and he continued breaking legal, moral, and spiritual laws, then walking up and down the aisle in church on Sunday with his arms raised up to God, blessing the people as though he was the Pope. The small church group brought their complaints to the pastor, and they were given his stock answer, "Take your un-forgiveness to the Cross."

The Report Splits The Church
The frustrated and distraught church group in his office took it upon themselves to conduct a thor-

ough investigation of the Pastor and Chief Elder. The more they dug, the more shocked they were, and their findings leaked throughout the congregation like an aggressive cancer. This led to a division in the church right down the center, so now you had two groups, the PROs (for the Pastor and Chief Elder) the ANTIs (against the Pastor and Chief Elder).

The PROs did not know the difference between evaluating and judging. Any adverse opinion about the Pastor and Chief Elder was viewed as judging God's Anointed. Their blanket motto for everything was "Judge not lest ye be judged." They considered it a godly obligation and a sign of great faith to accept anything the Pastor and Chief Elder said or did, after all, "they were God's appointed ones."

ANTIs believed that "By their fruit ye shall know them." In other words, if the Pastor and Chief Elder's thinking and behavior are not in line with the Scriptures, maybe they shouldn't be heading a church.

The two groups became more and more distant and coldly polite to each other. They sat on opposite sides of the center aisle. Where you sat pretty well indicated your position in the matter. I remember looking over the congregation and thinking of the Scripture that says, "A house divided shall surely fall."

Many offenses were endured silently by church victims, but as more and more unsavory news emerged, the ANTIs began admitting things more openly. One ANTI was a bank manager whom the Chief Elder had duped into getting a loan for him because he had such bad credit, but then he defaulted on the loan. She kept it to herself until this time. Another ANTI was his secretary. He withheld taxes on his workers, but never sent the money to the IRS. I don't quite understand it, but somehow, when the IRS came after him, the Chief Elder blamed her, and she became liable for his tax debt. Fortunately—or unfortunately—she was so poor there wasn't much they could get from her. The complaints continued to pour in from the ANTIs, and the case against this Demonic Duo was gaining momentum.

The more the Pastor's history was being investigated, the more he tried to put a stop to it. The church was being turned into a Mafia-like structure, with the Pastor as the Don and the Chief Elder as the Hit Man. When the Pastor put out the word, the Chief Elder tried to strong-arm the person. When the person wouldn't leave the service, the Chief Elder would call in the police with bogus charges. Such actions were unheard of in a church. They may be more likely in a cult, which this church was rapidly beginning to resemble.

A Cult Background

Try as they will, the Demonic Duo could not stop the investigation. As the small church group dug into the Pastor's background, a frightening picture emerged. They traced his religious origin back to a cult that he had formed in the South that had disintegrated through infighting. His prior homosexual partners in the cult so despised him now, they willingly provided signed statements against him, describing his character and behavior. It also turned out that the two children were not his, but his wife's from a previous marriage. In fact, there was no evidence that a marriage had ever taken place with the woman he marched so majestically down the aisle with. It was all a front, as was their Christian walk.

The cult members that followed him north were appointed to the Board of the Little White Church by the Cult Pastor. This gave him majority votes. During the final shuffle, it was rumored that the parsonage was inches from being voted into the Pastor's name. Also, no one seemed to know what happened to the money in the building fund that mysteriously vanished. Finally, the most startling information was the fact that this pastor was never ordained; therefore *he was not a pastor at all*.

Report Sent to Church Authorities

All evidence of the investigation was documented in a hefty report and forwarded to the Central Church Headquarters out west. It was returned with a letter telling them to submit it to the State Synod. The group sent it to the State Synod, but it was rejected because it was not presented by a church official. The church officials, many of them personal appointments of the fake pastor, or blindly loyal to him, wouldn't even read the report.

Despite all of this evidence, it took great persistence to convince one church official, a man who had been with the church since its inception, to read the report and when he saw the charges, and checked the validity of these charges, he put his name on it and sent it to the Synod. The Synod would not address the sexual implications, but went directly to the most compelling charge: the man parading as a pastor was *never ordained*. The fake pastor was given three days to vacate the parsonage.

After the removal of the fake pastor and his entourage, the Chief Elder was asked to step down. It was easier for a camel to go through the eye of a needle than to get this man out of office. He had no friends. His whole identity was the power this office gave him over others, but without the Pastor upholding him, it was only a question of time before this self-appointed pope was forced to step down.

PROs vs. ANTIs

You would expect people to be grateful that an impostor was exposed so that dignity, integrity and holiness could be restored in the church, but they weren't. The PROs were enraged. They condemned the ANTI nucleus that had exposed the pastor. The good guys became the bad guys. It's hard to understand that sometimes people become so accustomed to their chains, they almost can't live without them. They couldn't handle freedom and independence, so when this bomb dropped on the church, it disturbed their misguided sense of security. They fled in all directions, like a school of disoriented fish. Some left the church for good, some left Christianity altogether, some cried for years, grieving the death of their bondage. It reminded me of the Hebrews in Exodus who were being led out of captivity to the Promised Land by Moses. In time, they began complaining and faulting him for the inconvenience of their flight. There was a certain security in slavery.

The ANTIs, like myself, simply relocated to other churches. All I could think was, so much for my one-year trip down memory lane.

Final Gathering

I will never forget the final church gathering in Fellowship Hall just before the pastor got the notice to vacate. The Chief Elder came sauntering over to me, like an overstuffed splay-footed walrus, with a smirk on his face and said, "Whatsamatter? Don'tcha love me anymore?" He was giddy with victory because he had succeeded in convincing people that I had asked him to do something illegal. He relished tainting my reputation even more, now, because I was an ANTI who sided with the church investigating group and one who contributed a letter to help build their case.

When he mocked me, I looked at him square in the eye and said "You know, you're a pathological liar." He just laughed. You cannot insult a mocker. They like attention, even if it comes in the form of insults. I don't think that he or the Pastor were capable of realizing the damage they were doing to people's lives. It was a game to them, an insidious game of Power and Control over people they secretly despised and looked down on for their simple faith and humility. They followed no rule of good or bad, only what worked for them.

No Humanity Gene

They reminded me of the case of the well-respected middle-age man in a quiet suburban town who dug a dungeon under his house where he would enslave an unsuspecting young girl. After several years of molestation, he'd set her free and replace her with another victim. The first one was only 14. After the fifth one, when he was finally found out, his attitude was unfathomable. When questioned, he said he saw nothing wrong with what he was doing. He justified it with "My wife died and I had needs." When the interviewer tried to evoke a little regret from him for what he did, or a little compassion for these girls, he countered with "I was very good to these girls. I never hurt them. I am a very good person."

There are people in this world who are missing a humanity gene. They have lost all sense of right and wrong. That's what I saw in this Pastor and Chief Elder. Both were missing a humanity gene. It is a frightening thing when people who are devoid of compassion or ethics take over a church and twist Scripture to guilt people into blind obedience. That's what we saw with the Jonestown massacre.

I left the church before it all hit the fan, but I happened to be driving by the parsonage one day as a huge moving van was loading the pastor's stuff. I just shook my head in disbelief. Somebody forgot to tell this faux-pastor that he didn't have to fake it, that he had leadership qualities that could have been used for Good. A few years later, I heard he had died, and I don't think he was even 40. It didn't surprise me. You can't hurt so many decent people and not have God's judgment on your head.

Church Bottoms Out Again

After the pastor was evicted, the Chief Elder would not step down. He could not live without the power of that office and challenged them to make him leave before his term was up. It took a long time, but the board finally got him out. Strangely enough, he stayed in that church until he became an Elder again. What a mistake! I question the integrity of that board and I question whether this man even believed in God. In my opinion, he simply believed in power.

After going through a few pastors, the board finally found a man whose godly nature attracted many new people, and the membership grew. It became such a thriving church, that they considered moving to larger quarters.

I don't know if it was jealousy or what, but rumors were spreading that this demonic elder and his son drove the pastor out. I don't know exactly what happened, because it was ancient history to me, but all I know is that this pastor gave notice and left. After that, the church went downhill again and there were hardly enough members to even exist. The last I heard was that the board finally got wise to the Elder and his son, and they were ousted from the church. This should have been done years earlier, when the fake pastor was evicted. Why they let this Elder stay, and even made him an elder again, is beyond me. It's that old misinterpretation of "judging" and "evaluating." They didn't want to be guilty of judging, and they let an undesirable person stay long enough to lose a wonderful, godly pastor, and destroy the church. Now they know.

The one who suffered the most in this abysmal church catastrophe was the old singing pastor who had terrible misgivings about turning his church over to such bad people. He was such a good person, he did not recognize evil right under his nose.

Chapter II

The Inheritance

Once again, Karen's prophesy proved to be accurate, but God heard my prayer about not wanting anyone to die to inherit land. As it turned out, my name was put on the deed within two years without a death, so it was legally mine before anyone had to die. I wasn't told for a long time that my name was on the deed, and I did not inherit the "Promised Land" for another two years.

God's timing was perfect. I did not inherit the land until the very week that the negligence case on Jim's death was settled. I inherited the house on a Monday and the negligence case was settled two days later. If it hadn't happened that way, I wouldn't have had the $80,000 for the Inheritance Tax on the property. God was certainly behind such perfect timing.

The house was in the center of a two-and-a-half acre flag lot, not visible from the road. Even though it was in a very beautiful, affluent town, not far from where I was living, I could not get myself to move there. Not only was I reluctant to leave my safe medical building, but the house contained a chilling "presence" that made it impossible for me to stay there for more than a few minutes.

The "Presence"

The feeling is difficult to describe, except to say that it was sheer terror. Once, my son had opened a window to air out the house, and he called me to tell me to go there and shut the window because it was beginning to rain. He was unaware of my dread. I went there with great trepidation and quickly rushed over to the open window. It was stuck. That terrifying chill surrounded me and in a panic-stricken surge of strength, I slammed the window shut, almost breaking it, then fled from the house in a cold sweat panic.

This force was very disturbing and puzzling to me. What was it doing in a house owned and lived in by an elderly Christian couple, a house where there were prayer meetings every Monday night for years? I had planned to use it as the headquarters of a ministry, but how could I do this if I couldn't even step in the door? I agonized over the problem.

"You gave me a house, Lord," I cried. "How did such an evil presence get in there and how am I ever going to move in?"

I was not the only one that fled from this chilling "presence." Two other people, on separate occasions, ran out of the house. My son's friend said, "I'm never going back there again!" and the electrician said, "I gotta get outta here," and he rushed out with me trailing behind him. It was an eerie circus.

Despite such compelling evidence, I tried to tell myself that we were all imagining things, that it must be hysterics of some sort, so I decided to try one more thing. Mary, a friend of mine from the Little White Church, agreed to spend the night there with me to dispel this "myth." We went there with open minds to see if this "thing" was real or a figment of my imagination.

It turned out to be a nightmare that neither one of us will ever forget. The "presence" haunted the two of us and we got no sleep at all. Still, we stubbornly forced ourselves to stay the night. We left thoroughly exhausted and defeated, like it was a crime scene that couldn't be solved. The only thing gained was that there was now a witness to my contention that there was something cold and evil in that house.

The Exorcism

After two years of agonizing and praying earnestly about this "Promised Land," my fear changed to anger. The more I thought about it, and analyzed it, the more I realized that the "presence" didn't really do anything; it just terrorized. It didn't seem to have the power to harm me, but just to drive me away. I reasoned that IT just wanted the house to itself. What if it's only power was to say 'boo' and scare people away? That makes it a bully, and I do not like a bully, no matter what plane it's on.

It angered me further to think that it was not only blocking my gift from God, but God was not doing anything about it. Didn't Deuteronomy 28:8 say, "He shall bless thee in the land which the Lord, thy God, giveth thee." Where is my blessing if I can't set foot there?

Then I read about Moses. He sought God's help when he was leading the Israelites to the Promised Land, and God said, "Why do you cry out to Me? (You) Tell the children of Israel to go forward. Lift up your rod and stretch out your hand over the sea and divide it." Exodus 14:15. In other words, God

had already given Moses the power and it was up
to Moses to act on that God-given power. I thought
about that. As heirs to God's Kingdom, He has
already given us power over evil, so it was up to me
to use my God-given power to get that evil thing out
of my "Promised Land."

With this realization growing in my spirit, my
faith mushroomed. Then it seems that all sermons
that I heard at the time had to do with "possessing
your land." Finally, it all came to a head. It was time.

Fearlessly, with a Bible in my hand, I stormed the
house and took charge. I went from room to room
shouting "I don't know who you are, or what you
are doing here, but you can't stay! God gave me this
house and it belongs to me, and I want you out of
here!"

I opened the back door and shouted, "Out! In the
name of Jesus! Get OUT of my house . . . NOW!"

The cold chill instantly departed. To make sure
it did not come back once I left, I put a radio in
every room, upstairs and downstairs, all tuned in
to a Christian station. I figured that no evil spirit
can endure listening to sermons around the clock. It
would *want* to stay away.

Moving In

On the day I moved in, there was one final attempt
by the evil bully to frighten me. Just as I was ready to
go to bed, the electricity mysteriously blew and I sat
there in total darkness. There was no reason for this
to happen. There was no storm and no electrical construction going on anywhere, nothing. And it wasn't

just one circuit that blew; it was the whole house. Fear began to rise in me as I realized that I would have to go downstairs in the dark and make my way to the farthest corner to get to the circuit box. Then I got mad and said, "No, I will not be controlled by this bully. If God is for me, who can be against me?" With renewed faith, I felt my way down the stairs in the pitch black, all the way to the circuit breaker, saying, "Don't waste your time, demon. God's Word says that the Name of Jesus makes you tremble, so in the Name of Jesus, I claim your final removal. Get out and don't come back again!" I opened the electrical panel and ran my fingers up and down the switches. There wasn't one thing out of place. Then I turned the main switch off then on. The power came back on.

The evil presence was out of the house for good, although it did ring my back doorbell once. Fortunately, a friend was visiting, so there was a witness. I could see the door clearly through the picture window in the kitchen while the bell was ringing, and there was no one there. At least it was on the outside, not the inside. I simply said, "Don't even waste your time, because you're not coming in." The atmosphere in the house was so "clear" that the people who had fled in the past were eventually able to enter again, and even Mary came to visit many times. The "presence" was gone.

When I looked back on that strange occurrence against the backdrop of what happened later, I understood God's purpose in having me handle the problem myself. He knew that if I could handle the unseen, I could certainly handle the seen, because behind all evil, invisible and visible, there lurks the same spirit. God was preparing me for what was to come.

Chapter III

The Addition

Finally, I moved into my Promised Land in obedience to God's leadings, but my heart was, and still is at times, in my medical building. Though some of the worst experiences of my life happened while I lived there, it was also the place of my greatest experiences. I was living there when God staged the miraculous reunion between my daughter and her father. I was living there when I heard the voice of God. I was living there when Karen prayed life back into me and gave me all the powerful prophesies for my life. Living in that medical building was like childbirth. Once the beauty came, I forgot all about the pain.

After living in the Promised Land for a few years, I decided to build an addition, a little chapel. I wanted a special place where I, and perhaps others, could pray, like our own wailing wall. Four years had passed since my last encounter with the Chief Elder at Fellowship Hall, when he spoke those sarcastic words, "What's the matter? Don'tcha love me anymore?" That was all behind me and I was at the brink of a new life. I would now have my own chapel.

I had my blueprint and all my permits, and the Building Inspector was working closely with me. Everything was progressing nicely. Shortly into this project, the A-bomb struck. The building inspector happened to mention something about the Zoning Official, and who was the Zoning Official? It was none other than the evil Chief Elder. As soon as I heard this, a cold chill went through me. I *knew* there was going to be trouble. And it didn't take very long for it to appear.

The ZO Inspection
Almost immediately, the Zoning Official—nee Chief Elder—got wind of my construction and paid a sneak visit. Instead of coming during normal business hours, he came on a Sunday morning when he knew I would be in church. When have you ever heard of a town official making an inspection on a Sunday in his good clothes? There had to be strong motivation behind that. He did not expect that my son would be doing some work on the property, so I learned of his visit when I got home from church.

Fake Violations
Two days later, an official letter on municipal stationery came from his office citing nine false violations. In hindsight, I could see that he was as arrogant in local government as he was in the church because he had the protection of the highest power available. In the church it was the pastor, and in government, it was the mayor. He knew how to ingratiate himself to evil leaders and they needed each other. They needed him to do their bidding, and he needed them for power.

One violation was that there was only 12" below the sub-flooring instead of 15. The addition was a shell with exterior walls and roof, and doors that were locked. Had he been able to get in, he would have only had to lift a panel of plywood sub-flooring to see the 3 ft crawl space below. It was a total lie.

Another violation was that I had ordered four gas meters with intentions of making the property a multiple dwelling. He apparently didn't realize that it was an all-electric house. Nonetheless, I checked with the gas company in case the contractor made an error of some sort. They didn't even know what I was talking about. There was no such order.

I had some firewood for my and my son's fireplace out in the field, and another violation was that I was using the property as a transfer station for wood. I still am not sure what a transfer station is. Maybe because it was transferred to my son's house? I still don't know.

The rest of the violations were equally nonsensical. In addition to all the phony charges, he revoked every permit issued by the Building Inspector. When the Building Inspector read the charges, he said to me, "What on earth did you do to the Zoning Official to make him come after you like this? This is overkill!"

I said, "I helped expose him as a liar in a church matter, and this is payback." Now I understood why he asked for my survey in my last place and was so concerned about my occupying the medical building. I was right. He was not thinking as an Elder, he was thinking as a Zoning Official, and that's exactly what I said in my letter to the pastor. It also explains my sudden visit from that town's Zoning Official. This guy *did* report me, and was probably dismayed when I was allowed to live there.

The Building Inspector shook his head in disbelief. I could tell from his demeanor that he was very concerned for me. He was familiar with the arrogance of the Zoning Official and knew what he could do to me, a widow with no political connections. I didn't even know who was mayor. It's a good thing I didn't know what was coming down the road, or I might have fled back to my safe medical building. It was also a good thing that the Zoning Official didn't know what God had in store for him, or he would *never* have come after me.

The Letter To Mayor & Council

I naively assumed, as I did in the church, that those in authority would want to rectify a town situation, so, the way I wrote the pastor, I wrote a letter to the mayor and council. I explained that these charges were false and were the result of a grudge that grew out of a church conflict. I brought the letter to the municipal building and had the Borough Administrator place one in the mayor's and each councilman's box.

The First Anonymous Call

The first of a series of anonymous calls came as soon as I got back home. The man said "After you left the municipal building, the Borough Administrator read your letter. He immediately removed them from the boxes and threw them all in the wastebasket." When I heard that, I made copies and delivered them to the homes of the mayor and councilmen. I was never political and I had no idea how dangerous it was to confront politicians. If there ever was an ignorant person shaking up a hornet's nest, it was me.

After that, history repeated itself. The plot was the same, the characters were the same, but the setting was different. It was now the Mayor instead of the Pastor; the Zoning Official instead of the Chief Elder; and the Council instead of the Church Board, but the behavior of both groups was indistinguishable. No one was interested in truth, only power and control. You were not supposed to question authority, but simply obey. Right or wrong, you are wrong, and without God's help, there is no way to fight such people. You can't win on your own.

Borough Attorney Enters

The matter of my violations was turned over to the Borough Attorney who gave me ten days to correct the violations. I wrote back, "Do you have any suggestions on how to correct violations that don't exist?" My plea was misunderstood as arrogance, so he and the local government came down on my head like a giant goliath. A simple inspection would have resolved the matter, but none of those in power were interested. Everything the Zoning Official said was believed, and the matter was in the hands of the Borough Attorney.

Exodus 22:22-24

When you're alone and are at the mercy of unscrupulous people, especially one focused on "payback" and he has a whole local government behind him, including the Borough Attorney, it's time to pull out the Big Guns, so I opened the Bible and searched for an appropriate Scripture. I found Exodus 22:22-24. "You shall not afflict any widow or fatherless child. If you afflict them in any way and they cry at all to Me, I will surely hear their cry; and My wrath will become hot, and I will kill you with the sword." I figured that Scripture will do, and I called upon God daily with this Scripture to help me

The Honest Building Inspector
The Borough Attorney sent a copy of the Zoning Official's letter to the Building Inspector for his comments, fully expecting corroboration, but the Building Inspector would not perjure himself. He knew that everything was legal and to-code, so he answered all of the charges honestly. (Here's where God came in.) He then slipped me a copy of the charges with his hand written comments to the right of each charge—without the town's knowledge or permission. Every answer rebutted the charges, including the fact that the Zoning Official did not have the authority to revoke permits issued by a Building Inspector. Of course, the Borough Attorney did not know that I had seen this rebuttal and continued to act as though they had the goods on me, that I had broken zoning laws. The Borough Attorney continued to send dunning letters and more summonses.

The Stop Order
The Zoning Official did not honor God's laws when he was Chief Elder, so why would he honor

man's laws as Zoning Official? He was above the law, therefore, when the Building Inspector refused to post a Stop Order on my addition, he took it upon himself to do it. Naturally, this scared off the last of my construction crew, so everything came to a halt, even though I had already paid a second time for all permits. It was really hopeless. They were going to get me no matter what. But they did not know that help was on the horizon. God was on His way.

The Mayor, The Boss

In a Mayor and Council form of government, the council has the power and the mayor has the power to break a tie and chair the meetings. That wasn't so in this town. Twenty years earlier, when the mayor entered politics, he hand picked his own council and either they listened to him, or they were gone, so he was surrounded by yes-men. They did what *he* said. The mayor became more and more powerful over the years so that he began to think of the town as his personal fiefdom. No one ever ran against him and no one dared question anything he did. He also hand-picked the Zoning Official and was planning to have him take over the whole building department as soon as he passed the State exams, so the fix was in. I didn't stand a chance against all this power. However, *they* didn't stand a chance against the real power of the universe, but they didn't know it.

Letters To The Editor

I sought justice at council meetings, but the local government was hostile and rude. When I opened my mouth to speak, the mayor used the gavel to silence me. They saw me as the enemy and I didn't know which way to turn. But I *had* to do *something*. After much prayer, I was impressed to bring my plight to the people. I start a writing campaign through Letters To The Editor and openly aired every injustice that was being done to me. The mayor was absolutely furious, and inspections and summonses doubled.

People were afraid to buck this mayor, because they knew he'd stop at nothing, even go after your job. If I had a nine-to-five job, it would have been over for me, but I didn't. As a piano technician, I didn't know, myself, where I would be from day to day, so his hands were tied.

The Fall Prophesied

The Zoning Official did exactly what he did in the last town, he promoted slander against me. My friend, Mary, from the Little White Church, and I passed the Zoning Official at a parking lot one day. He glared at me and said, "At least I never stole a house." Mary stopped in her tracks, turned, and shouted in a loud, prophetic voice, "YOU WILL FALL BY YOUR LIES!" It was like a pronouncement from the voice of God. I will never forget it.

Even though people knew the character of this Zoning Official, there are some who believed him. His accusation implied that I put a pen in a dying person's hand and made them sign something to get the house. Had they gone to the courthouse, they would see for themselves that my name was added to the deed long before anyone died. Unfortunately, there are a few people that may still believe this lie, but I can't worry about them.

This rumor may have been what gave fuel to this mayor and council to come after me so viciously. They must have believed that I stole the house. It all made sense, now. However, the Zoning Official, not satisfied that he spread a vicious lie about me, he went a step further and called the ZO in the town I had left, where I still owned the house and medical building. It was now five years after the church matter, and he was *still* spreading that old lie that I wanted him to build an illegal addition. This man was always doing mischief, but his deeds were reported right back to me, and it would end up in the newspapers.

That other ZO, I think his name was Tony, called me up and reported that the Zoning Official who reported me was an s.o.b. who belongs in jail. He also told me that he took that wayward Zoning Official to court for violations and won. The Zoning Official was no champion among his peers. Maybe the church people were naïve and believed his lies, but experienced officials knew better. They knew his reputation and told me to be careful, that this Zoning Official was an insidious snake—as if I didn't know it.

People Rallied

Once I began airing my complaints in the newspapers, it unleashed a battery of anonymous calls and letters by people who were victimized by this Zoning Official and they wanted to help me expose him. Even his neighbors hated him and called me. I was overwhelmed by the response. He owed everybody money, artisans, laborers, and suppliers, for his construction company. Someone even sent me his tax returns anonymously, returns that showed he owed the government thousands of back taxes in three different names; two businesses, and himself.

Artisans called and told me that the Zoning Official built an addition on his house five years earlier and he did not get all the permits, nor inspections, and had no CO, so he paid no tax on it, though it was completed. They listed all the illegal work that the Zoning Official had them do that ignored building codes, all the things that he issued summonses for to other residents. The reason why these artisans were still angry is that the ZO never paid them, not one of them. I thought about what these hardworking men told me and realized that the ZO was doing all of his illegal building during the time he was telling people that *I* asked *him* to do something illegal. Not only that, he did them while he was Chief Elder in the church, walking up the aisle in the church, blessing the people like he was the Pope. Doesn't a person like this believe there is a God? That you reap what you sow? If there ever was a person who was asking for God's vengeance, it was this man.

The Zoning Official's Violations Denied

I stood before the mayor at the next council meeting and asked "What are you going to do about the Zoning Official's violations?"

Two councilmen jumped up and said, "I don't have to listen to this!" and they stormed off the dais and left. The mayor added, "If I weren't chairing this meeting, I'd leave, too."

No one had ever challenged this local government before, and they couldn't take it. One word from me, and the whole meeting fell apart. Despite their hostile behavior, I continued. I was not thrilled at going before this governing body, but what choice did they give me?

Again I asked, "What are you going to do about the Zoning Official's violations on his own house?"

The mayor's profound answer was, "The Zoning Officer is the Zoning Officer." That was an answer?

I asked a third time what they were going to do about the violations on the Zoning Official's house, and the mayor's glib answer was, "I was advised by the building department that everything was inspected, and it was not inspected by our inspectors, it was inspected by outside ones." I knew it was all a lie.

When I asked when this inspection took place, he said, "I really don't have to answer that question," and he quickly aborted our dialogue with, "I'm not going to discuss it any further. Your time is up."

I remember feeling like I hit a brick wall. I knew the mayor was lying, but what could I do about it? I didn't know enough to fight this man. You don't learn anything about local government when you are tuning pianos, so I didn't know what to do next. However, I continued to pray about the matter, asking God to help me, and I noticed that every time

I prayed about it, the answer would mysteriously show up.

God Sends Help

The next morning, my excavator came by to pick up his huge backhoe that was sitting on my property, and he asked me how things were going. I said, "Well, I don't really know what to do. I was told that there were violations on the Zoning Official's house, and I brought it before the council last night, and the Mayor said that everything was inspected by outside inspectors. I know it's not true, but how can I prove it?"

He said, "Why don't you go over to the building department and look at the records?"

I was astounded. "Am I allowed to do that?" I couldn't believe it.

"Of course. Records are public information. They can't refuse you."

"What will these records tell me?"

"They will tell you if the Zoning Official had the proper permits to build, and when the legal rough and final inspections took place."

After this man left, I thanked God for this information, and I decided to go to the municipal building right then and there. Knowing that I was dealing with a whole bunch of liars, I decided to record as much as I could from now on so I could put it in the newspapers.

I had a pocketbook that was shaped like a horse's feed bag, with an open top. It was perfect for a tape recorder. Armed and ready, I went to the Municipal

Building. I knew so little, I didn't know that I could go directly to the Building Department, but thought I had to check in at the front desk first.

Violating The Right To Know law

The Borough Administrator came over uneasily and scowled, "Can I help you?" I placed my pocketbook with the running tape recorder on the counter right under his mouth, and said, "I'd like to look at the Zoning Official's building records."

He answered, "It's against town policy."

He was breaking the Right To Know Law right into the tape. I wasn't feeling as helpless as the night before, so I looked right into his eyes and watched him break the law. I was the cat, now, waiting for the mouse to run. I wondered how he would react when he sees his words in next week's newspaper.

With bold and reckless confidence, he said, "Look, I'll show you. Follow me," and he led me downstairs to the Building Department. He explained to the Building Inspector that I wanted to look at the Zoning Official's building records, but that I needed to know that it was against town policy. He expected the Building Inspector to back him up and say that it was against the town policy to open the building records to residents.

Instead, the Building Inspector looked him right in the eye and said, "You know I can't do that. I just got a flyer from the State today to be posted on the board. It was sent to remind towns that that these building records must be open to the public." This answer made the Borough Administrator shake with rage.

I didn't help the situation any when I said to the Borough Administrator, "Just in case you're afraid that I'll steal something, have the Building Inspector bring the records, and I'll put my hands behind my back, and *you* turn the pages."

The Borough Administrator was so angry, his ears turned crimson. Without a word, he swung around and stomped off, slamming every door on the way to his office. It sounded like thunder overhead.

Mayor On The Alert

The Administrator immediately called the mayor who pulled all inspectors off their jobs and sent them over to the Zoning Official's property. This action belies his statement the night before that the Zoning Official's property had already been inspected by outside inspectors. Also, for him to call these inspections, he apparently thought they would disprove my allegations.

Knowing that this powerful mayor had everyone in his pocket, I didn't expect much from these inspectors, but I was wrong. I learned that only the Zoning Official answers to the mayor. The Construction, Electrical, Fire Code, and Plumbing Inspectors answer to the State, not to the Mayor, and they are not about to put their license at risk for a dishonest Mayor. This is probably why the mayor wanted his Zoning Official to take over the whole building department. This would give him more power.

Also, my letters in the newspapers were distressing the mayor and council. They didn't want the residents at large to know what was going on. People were reacting and the mayor was beginning to sweat. The tables were turned, and instead of my being afraid of them, they were afraid of me. Only God can do that!

The Zoning Official's Violations Confirmed
A copy of these inspections was sent me anonymously, and I had to shake my head in disbelief. This Zoning Official, who was going after me like a ravenous wolf, had more violations than anyone he cited. He had built an addition with plumbing, electrical, zoning, and fire code violations. He built a deck without a permit; he built it over a septic tank; the plumbing was illegal; indoor electrical sockets were used outdoors, which was illegal; there was no permit to put up a fence, and no variance to put up the 6ft fence that he installed; there was an unregistered car on the premises; there were piles of debris around the property; and no complete fence around the pool. Apart from one rough electrical inspection five years earlier, there were no other rough or final inspections. He never got a Certificate of Occupancy and thereby avoided paying taxes on an addition that he had already occupied for five years.

After putting this in the newspapers, I went before the mayor and council and asked again what they were going to do about the Zoning Official's violations, and the mayor's angry answer was, "Nothing!

The work is ongoing!" Politicians lie so easily, it's in their DNA and job description.

The mayor was so eager to retaliate after seeing my newspaper article, he sent an official to check on the Zoning Official's statement that I had ordered four gas meters. The official returned to him and said, "There's not even one." This mayor did his best to get me, but there was nothing to get.

Concerns For My Safety

Having the mayor, the council, the Borough Administrator, the Borough Attorney, and the ZO after me, all men with no particular ethics, people were concerned about my safety. They told me that I would never be able to stand up to such powerful people. But I said, "That's what they told David in the Bible when he was on his way to kill the giant with nothing more than a slingshot?" I told them, "I have a slingshot, too: my pen."

I was empowered with a strong belief that if God is for you, who can be against you? I simply kept the matter in prayer and in the newspapers, and believed that God was guiding me and protecting me.

It was no accident that there was an anonymous underground army that reported every move of the enemy to me, so I always knew everything that was going on. I suspected that most of the calls came from within the local government, because I was informed not only of what was happening within the town, but also what was happening within the Municipal Meetings. I was always well-informed.

The Man With The Trees

Another case reached my ears. Louis was a very rich young man who was a talented designer with a prosperous business in New York. He lived down the street from one of the councilman in the most exclusive part of town. As it was told to me, the old councilman was so jealous of the young millionaire, he sent the Zoning Official there to hand out summonses, and we know that if an inspector is after you, he'll find a reason for the summonses.

The rich man was beautifying his property and had paid a hundred thousand dollars for 6' trees that needed to be planted. While the trees were lying on their side, along came the Zoning Official who put a Stop Order on the sprinkler system that he claimed was a few inches too short so violated the code. Every time the man tried to water the trees so they wouldn't die, out pounced the Zoning Official from the bushes. By the time I learned of this case, the man had 22 summonses, had hired an attorney, and the case was pending.

I went brazenly to Louis' house. To keep the Zoning Official off their property, they had now installed a wrought iron fence around the whole property, so you had to speak into the mailbox before you could get in. They knew my name from the newspapers, and buzzed me through their 6 ft iron gate. We sat on their stone porch and he told me their tale of horror. I had such an inner sense that God was with me that I vowed to him and his wife, then and there, that this Zoning Official will be brought down. I held fast to Exodus 22:22-24 and knew that God was not pleased with what this Zoning Official and the local government were doing to me and to others. When you think of it objectively, how brave can a bunch of men be who join forces to bring down a 5ft widowed piano tuner?

A Barnacle
This Zoning Official reminded me of a barnacle. A barnacle has no power in itself, so it attaches itself to something else, like a shark or a whale, something that has power. The Zoning Official, as Chief Elder, attached himself to the power in the church—the pastor—so he could gain power vicariously and control those below him. Given power, he could say or do anything to people with impunity. He loved condemning people and making them feel unworthy. He preyed on religious people's sense of guilt and enjoyed doling out blessings as a self-appointed pope.

And in the town, he attached himself to the highest power, the Mayor, so he could bully people and wield his unjust power without having to give an account to anyone for his own infractions. Well, I figured he had gone too far, now. It was time to send this barnacle to a sunken ship.

Wasted Potential
The Zoning Official had a very bright future when he was Chief Elder in the Little White Church. The fake pastor was grooming him for the lucrative position of Faith Healer, which made me laugh when I heard it. If he didn't have the power to heal my ear, what was he going to do when he was confronted

with cancer? It was obviously going to be a scam to rake in the big bucks. I could see him praying for people, and when they were not healed, he would say, "You just didn't have enough faith."

And the mayor was grooming him, as Zoning Official, to take over the whole building department as combined Construction Official, Zoning Official, plus extra services, such as Recycling Agent.

Even though the Faith Healer angle failed after the pastor was evicted, he still had the potential of earning at least $113,000 as combined Building Inspector/Zoning Official of the whole Building Department in town. At that time, $113,000 was a great deal of money. It would be equal to at least three-four times that today. But I knew that if this ZO took over the whole building department, it would spell disaster not only for me, but for all residents. Give a guy like that power and control, and he'll destroy the morale of a whole town.

I wanted to do something to stop this ruthless official from taking over the whole Building Department, but I didn't know how. Since the mayor had appointed him Zoning Official, I thought it was the Mayor who would appoint him as Construction Official/Zoning Official, so I couldn't go to the Mayor. He would never listen to me. I didn't know what to do next; but as usual, when I needed to know something, God would send the right person.

Community Affairs

One of the anonymous callers told me that it's the Department of Community Affairs that issues

Construction Official licenses for a State, not the
Mayor. That news offered hope to the situation. I
could circumvent the local government and go right
to the State. And God certainly intervened in my call
to the State.

The man I called at Community Affairs was out
to lunch and a young boy was manning the phones.
I asked him questions about our Zoning Official and
he pulled out the application and read the whole
application to me. I'm not sure he was supposed to
give out that information, and had the boss been
there, I am certain he would not have given me so
much information.

I was told that to become combined Construction
Official/Zoning Official, you have to pass three
exams, and the ZO had already passed two and had
applied for the third exam that very month. One
of the questions asked on the application was if the
applicant had ever been convicted of a felony, and
the Zoning Official checked No.

Earlier that month, I had received an anonymous
call from a court in another town. I was told that our
Zoning Official had been found guilty of passing bad
checks, a felony. The judge threw out the false coun-
terclaims against the plaintiff, because they were all
lies. In other words, in the very month that the Zoning
Official was convicted of passing bad checks, he lied
on his application with the State to take that third
and final exam to qualify as combined Construction
Official/Zoning Official by saying he had never been
convicted of a felony.

Community Affairs Steps In

Naturally, I put it in the newspaper, and the Zoning Official scrambled for alibis. He said that his attorney told him that passing bad checks was a "disorderly persons" charge, not a felony, so he didn't feel that he needed to report it on his application. Nobody bought that, especially not Community Affairs. I followed the example of the small church group whose investigation brought down a false pastor. I documented everything that happened. I made tapes where I could, saved all newspaper articles, and when the other venue sent the court records back to our town, I made copies of the convictions and added them to my expanding file. Practically every move concerning the Zoning Official was taped right from the source, so it was virtually impossible for the ZO to refute the charges.

The initial letter from the Zoning Official was sent me the beginning of May, and it was now July. It was time to send all evidence to the State, just as the small investigating group in the Little White Church sent their report to the Synod. I had taped the artisans and officials and building inspectors from other towns saying that this Zoning Official was an unregenerate thief and liar who belonged in jail. I included a copy of the fake charges against me, the copy that included the Building Inspector's comments that exonerated me; the court records of his bad check charges and conviction, a copy of the building records on his own house that showed he didn't follow the building codes himself. Every single piece of evidence that I could get my hands on went to the State.

Six weeks later, the State sent a representative to investigate the matter. The man interviewed officials in the municipal building one by one, and no one had a good word to say about the Zoning Official. The investigator inspected my addition, and you could see the disgust on his face over the false charges. He could only shake his head, but not comment openly. He checked out every charge the ZO made against me, and every charge that I made against him. He checked out the court files, where the bad check charges were now recorded on our town records.

The Judgment

By October 14, after six months of steady harassment by the Zoning Official and local government, endless nonsensical inspections of my property, endless warning letters, and endless summonses, it all came to a head.

The Bible says "Their swords will enter their own hearts," and that's exactly what happened. The State handed down a Judgment against the Zoning Official on two charges:

1) Posting an unauthorized Stop Order on my construction; and

2) Lying on his application about his conviction.

With this, the Zoning Official lost his legal right to ever become Construction Official in the whole state. What's more, the mayor and council were forced to dismiss him. As angry as the Zoning Official was at the news, the mayor was angrier. Where was he going to find himself another ambitious official like this one?

Community Affairs sent me a copy of the Judgment, and returned all of my evidence. The first thing I did was to give a copy of the Judgment to the rich man with the trees and twenty-two summonses. It was presented to his judge and the case plus all of his summonses were thrown out.

The Wages of Sin

The mayor provided the Borough Attorney to handle the Zoning Official's Appeal—at taxpayers' expense—but it failed. There was really no defense. Psalm 37 says, "When the wicked are cut down, you shall see it." And I saw it! By trying to destroy me, the Zoning Official destroyed himself. He lost his job; his house went into foreclosure; and he was banned from ever working in local government again in the whole state. When God says not to afflict a widow, He means it. Leave the widow alone! Don't look for trouble! I wasn't bothering anyone. My construction was legal and up-to-code, so why did he have to come after me with such a vengeance?

Zoning Official Trashes House

Anonymous calls continued to come in. I was told that after the Zoning Official lost his house, he moved his family into a rental in the next town, then went back to the foreclosed house with a sledge hammer and trashed the whole inside. What a pity! All of that illegal construction for nothing.

Mayor Punishes Fire Code Inspector

After that, the Mayor was on a vicious warpath. He wouldn't give up. He ordered the Fire Code Official to issue me a summons.

"What for, Mayor?"

"Because Joyner had a fireplace on her blueprint, but didn't build it."

"Mayor, I issue summonses when people DO something, not when they DON'T do something."

As a result, the mayor did what was his standard pattern. If you didn't do what he said, you got punished, usually in your pocketbook. He cut the Fire Code Official's hours, causing a financial loss for him from then on.

The Mayor Punishes The Construction Official

The Mayor was so incensed that the Construction Official refused to violate the Right To Know law and allowed me to see the Zoning Official's building records, and refused to put a Stop Order on my addition, the mayor refused to renew the Construction Official's contract. The CO was ready to retire and had been promised one more year so that his pension would kick in, but he was fired, instead. Sadly, the Construction Official had taken out a $30,000 loan on the basis of this promise, and found himself out of a job with loan payments. I often wondered what happened with the pension.

I don't know if the Mayor did anything to all of those officials who were truthful in their inspection report on the Zoning Official and when the State Investigator questioned them about the Zoning

Official. I guess he couldn't fire everyone. He and his council cronies couldn't run a town from an empty municipal building.

The Strong Man Runs

I cannot end this chapter without mentioning that I ran into the ex-Zoning Official one more time a month after he was fired. He had moved to the next town where I did my food shopping. I was pushing my cart along the aisle of the supermarket one evening. Coming toward me from the opposite direction was the ex-Zoning Official, also pushing a cart. The moment he saw me, he stopped in his tracks, swung his cart around and literally fled, still pushing his cart.

For some unexplainable reason, I took off after him, and it turned into high speed shopping cart chase. But there was no catching up to him. He abandoned his cart recklessly and then flew out the front door.

I don't know why he was so afraid. I was only going to say what he said to me the last time he saw me at church, "Whatsamatter? Don'tcha love me anymore?"

Chapter IV

The Horse

At The Crossroads

A few months before the Zoning Official situation was resolved, a young woman came to me, crying. The Morgan Mare given her as a child was now 25 years old, swayback and blind. She loved riding, so bought a younger horse, but could not find it in her heart to put down her old mare. However, it became too much of a financial burden to board two horses, so she found herself at a devastating crossroad. She didn't want to give up the new horse, but she couldn't bear the thought of putting her old horse down, so she was sobbing.

According to the animal code in my town, you need one acre for a house and one acre for a horse. With two and a half acres, my property more than complied with the ordinance, so I told her that if she covered expenses, she could keep Lia on my property free of charge. She was overjoyed. We would share all chores and she would come on Saturdays to groom her. I can't think of a horse that got better care than Lia. Between the owner and me, Lia was pet and pampered and brushed and sprayed. The vet and the farrier came regularly to check her so she was in great shape for an old mare.

It may not have been the wisest thing to apply for a horse permit while battling the Zoning Official over an addition, but it couldn't be put off. It was a matter of life and death for the horse. Our plan was to bring Lia to my property on October 1, but before this, the Health Official had to OK everything. At the direction of the mayor, he put up as many road blocks as he could.

Applied For Permit

When I applied for a permit to keep a horse, the Health Official said I had to have a shed. We built a shed. Then he said that it had to be a barn. We enlarged it into a two-stall barn, one side for Lia, and the other side as a tack room. The Construction Official oversaw the construction and it was to code. Then the Health Official said you didn't need any structure at all, but that there had to be grass in the paddock. We put up a corral fence and spread grass seed in the paddock. There were endless inspections and delays. Finally, by September they ran out of obstacles and Lia's owner covered the $25 license fee and the permit was issued.

Lia Arrives Late

For some reason, I can't remember why, but Lia could not be moved till October 20, but the town didn't know that and assumed that she would arrive on the First.

Once the State issued a Judgment against the Zoning Official for putting a Stop Order on my addition and for lying on his application about his conviction, all hell broke loose and it spilled onto the horse matter. The mayor was so enraged over losing the zoning battle to me and being forced to fire his right-hand man, he came after the horse.

Even though I complied with every single real and imaginary requirement they gave me to keep a horse, the harassment began. The Borough Administrator came up to me in the second week of October, right after they received the Judgment on the Zoning Official, to tell me that neighbors were complaining about the horse, that there was a foul smell and flies.

I answered him with feigned concern, "That's odd. The horse hasn't come, yet." His ears turned crimson, as they did when he could not get the Construction Official to close the building files to me, and he stomped off. I was beginning to think that crimson ears and the ability to stomp and slam doors were a part of his job description.

The Illegal Meeting

On October 30, ten days after Lia actually arrived, an anonymous caller informed me that the mayor called a five-minute meeting with the Health Official about my horse. This was illegal as they did not notify me and I was entitled to be at this meeting. The mayor produced a scathing letter for the Health Official to sign, but it was so bad, he refused. The Health Official agreed to write a more toned down letter saying that he had given me a permit in error, and that my property didn't qualify. The Health Department gave me ten days to remove the horse from my property and the new battle was launched.

Lia's New Battle

It was out of the question to remove Lia. She had been a faithful companion for years, and was such a sweet, gentle guest on my property. I never knew how intelligent and loving a horse could be. The minute I opened my back door, she'd call out to me in a beautiful whinny. It was music to my ears. We became great friends and I wasn't going to send this gentle old blind horse to the executioner. She earned the right to live her few remaining years in peace, and I intended to see that she got it. But the mayor saw it differently, and the harassment began. It was the Addition thing all over again, the lies, the inspections, and more summonses.

The Attorney

Lia's owner was willing to pay for an attorney, which was still cheaper than boarding a horse, so she was still ahead. The lawyer, a heavy drinker, was terrible, so terrible in fact, that a few years later, he was disbarred. At times I suspected that he was in league with the Borough Attorney, another inept lawyer, when he suggested that I remove Lia from the property "for now." I said no. Frankly, I preferred to remove the lawyer from the property than the horse "for now." Meanwhile, I made sure that their every move against the horse went into the newspapers.

An Attempt To Kill The Horse

During the drawn out battle, someone entered my property one Sunday while I was at church and tossed all the hay out of the tack room into the paddock. They then left Lia there to eat herself to death. A domestic horse will do that when surrounded by food. I got there just in time. First I put Lia in her stall, then I dragged the remaining bales of hay back into the tack room. The Vet came and poured a gallon of mineral oil down her throat to help her digest and pass the excess food. When the Vet left, I put an incident report on record with the police after they investigated and observed foreign footprints. My newspaper report of the incident got the attention of the Animal Rights people. They began to raise their voices for me. They even sent a flyer around that made my local government look very bad.

When the attempt on Lia's life failed, the local leaders tried something else. They never ran out of ideas, those scoundrels. The Engineer, who was now the Acting Zoning Official, called me into his office. He said, "According to the Horse Ordinance, there is a 25 foot setback around your whole property. When that setback is deducted, you do not have sufficient acreage to keep a horse."

I looked him in the eye and said, politely and calmly, "Would you please give me a copy of that Ordinance?"

He didn't know what to say. There was no such Ordinance.

The Horse Trial

After a year of inspections, summonses, an attempt on Lia's life, legal letters and lies, it was finally time to go to court. There was a change of venue, and after all my letters to the Editor, everyone, but everyone knew about the horse. People came from all over the county to observe the seven-hour trial. I suppose it was the biggest event in the area. It was even picked up by the county newspaper.

Our lawyer was useless—too bad he wasn't disbarred sooner—and it was the judge who did all the cross examining for my case.

The Engineer was useless in presenting the town's case as Acting Zoning Official. I actually felt a little sorry for him. He was neither an attorney nor a Zoning Official and he said and did everything wrong. He presented a hand-drawn diagram of my property that made the land look like a concrete parking lot in his effort to disqualify my property as pasture land. I presented pictures to disprove his diagram. It caused the judge to ask a lot of questions, questions that exposed a dishonest attempt to falsely describe my property.

The Acting Zoning Official tried everything he could think of. He tried to prove there wasn't enough land by disallowing the trees—and the trees were not even in the paddock.

The judge's response was, "Don't horses walk through woods?"

Then he tried to disallow the pond, which was at the entrance of the property, nowhere near the paddock, and the Judge said, "Don't horses drink from ponds?"

In other words, instead of having a drawing that proved the town's case, it contributed to winning mine by bringing up all these points.

The judge knew that this case was not about a horse, anyway. It was about the abuse of power that had crippled a potentially great town. My letters appeared not only in my area, but in all the surrounding towns, so everyone knew what was going on in my town.

By the time of the trial, the Health Official had resigned—I could see the Hand of God in that—and the new Health Official turned out to be a born-again Christian. I could see God's Hand in that, too. The old Health Official may have been willing to lie, I don't know. He knew that everything was legal with the horse but still agreed to sign a false letter stating that the permit was given in error. I felt certain that this Christian Health Official would not lie.

When the Health Official took the stand, the Judge asked him what the procedure was in renewing a permit.

He answered, "People send in their $25 and we send them their renewal."

"If Mrs. Joyner sent in her money, would you renew her permit?"

"No."

"Why not?"

"I'd have to bring it before the Board."

"Do you have to bring anyone else's before the Board?"

"No."

"Why would you have to bring Mrs. Joyner's renewal request before the Board."

"I'm sorry, I can't say."

This testimony revealed political prejudice against me and I'm sure it had weight in the judge's decision, but his ruling was specifically based on the fact that the town called a five-minute meeting to revoke my horse permit without notifying me.

The judge ordered that my permit be renewed.

The mayor was so obsessed with revenge after losing two cases to me that he was not willing to drop the matter and wanted to Appeal it. It wasn't about winning the Appeal, either; he knew he couldn't win. It was only a ploy to keep me paying legal fees. He thought he was hurting me, but he was hurting the horse's true owner. And he didn't care how long legal action would run; it didn't cost him a penny. The town would pay. So far, between all the inspections and letters and case preparation, and whatever, it was estimated that he had already spent Twenty to Twenty-Five Thousand Dollars to fight my $25 permit. Lia's owner paid only around a hundred a month, something like that.

But a strange thing happened.

A New Councilman

During my seemingly endless battle with the town, one of the councilmen either died or was ill or moved, I can't remember. They were all elderly men, so it could have been anything. He was replaced with a new councilman who was younger. Not only that, he was related to the Head of the Health Department. He had heard all the bad stories about me and sided with them for the entire time of the conflict.

When I heard about the possible Appeal, I knew that their argument was that my old horse was a problem to the neighbors. I decided to go straight to these neighbors to see how they felt about my horse.

We were all on large plots with thick trees between us, so I had to drive to the next block to get to the houses behind me. To my utter surprise, they didn't even know I had a horse. They couldn't see it, hear it, or smell it.

The first neighbor I went to had a great idea. She said, "Why don't you write up a petition and have us all sign it?" So that's what I did. The petition stated that there were no flies or odor and that the horse presented no problem to the neighborhood. I asked everyone around me to sign except for two neighbors. One was a friend of the mayor and the other was on a town board. I later found out that this neighboring official was asked to be involved in favor of the mayor, but he refused. He was an attorney, and didn't want to get involved in a town skirmish, so they left him alone, and he left me alone. We have never had a problem with each other, ever.

I sent copies of the signed petition to the mayor and council and invited them to inspect my property. No one responded. Then one evening at ten of seven, I got a call from the new councilman who said he would be coming by to inspect my property. Ten minutes later, he showed up with his wife and the Head of the Health Department. They walked back and forth and were truly amazed at how clean and sanitary everything was. That's not what they were expecting. They were told lies by the mayor and council, so he was expecting to see filth and flies. He was in utter shock.

After this visit, I never heard another word about the Appeal and the horse permit was issued. The matter was finally over.

The New Councilman Apologizes
Late one afternoon, I went for a slice of pizza in the next town, and I ran into the new councilman and his wife. He spent the next two hours or so apologizing to me over and over for believing the stories he was told.

"When I got on the council," he said, "I was like the new kid on the block. I believed what I was told and I supported such beliefs. But I began to see how lethal the mayor was, how spiteful, how petty, how vindictive and mean-spirited he was. He ordered not only the council, but the whole municipal building to not speak to you. When my wife and you had that brief chat after the last council meeting, the mayor took me aside and said 'I have your resignation in my pocket and will give it to the newspapers if you don't get better control of your wife.' "

If it hadn't been for this new councilman, the horse matter would have continued. He told me that after he inspected my land, he went back to the mayor and council, and told them "I find nothing wrong with Ms. Joyner's land and care of her horse, and neither does the Head of the Health Department. I say we put this matter behind us," and they did. That was God working through this new councilman.

The battle was over . . . but the war continued.

Chapter V

The Election

The Council Brotherhood

Two years had passed since the initial attack, a year for the addition matter and a year for the horse matter. The Zoning Official was gone, not only out of office but out of town, never to cross my path again. And with a renewed permit to keep a horse, Lia could now enjoy her remaining years in her private paddock unhampered. It was time, now, for some well-deserved peace and quiet. Then came the shocking anonymous call.

I was told that the mayor was seething. He was not used to losing, and he could not bear losing to me, a nobody, a nothing. He had won four elections unchallenged, and with each one, gained more and more power, power that he wielded like a self-absorbed Tsar. He was furious that he was forced to obey the law because in his mind, *he* was the Law.

In a normal government setup, there is a mayor and six councilmen. If the six council members vote on an issue and the result is a tie, the mayor has the power to break a tie. Apart from chairing the meeting and breaking a tie, the mayor is not the power in local government, the council is. But, like the fake pastor in the little white church, when you put your cronies in office, they do what you say and you have *absolute* power and can run things exactly the way you want.

The first council meeting I attended was an eye-opener. After the standard opening formalities plus a few minutes, I yawned, and when I came out of the yawn, they were adjourning. This group so agreed on everything, there was no reason to discuss anything. I remember saying, "That was it?" The meeting was no more than ten minutes, total.

When I caught onto the mayor and council brotherhood, I understood why none of the councilmen stepped forward to question the issues mentioned in my original letter about the zoning official. This council was a political demolition ball with the mayor operating the machine. They wore the mayor's footprints across their souls. Watching this group operate was a better education than a degree in Government.

Eminent Domain Threat

The battle that I thought was over was not over; it was just entering a new phase. The anonymous caller told me that the mayor was so furious that he had lost two battles to me, an insignificant widow, a piano tuner no less, that he was going to "get" me if it was the last thing he ever did. He talked of condemning my property under Eminent Domain in order to make it a park "for the good of the town." I was stunned.

I never heard of Eminent Domain. "Could he do that?"

"Yes."

"Would he do that?"

"You bet."

One of my earlier anonymous callers told me that he went all through elementary and high school with the mayor and said he was the student who never got the girl. That told me a lot. No wonder he was so angry and demanded so much power. I've heard it called the "small man's syndrome."

After much prayer, it came to me that this mayor had to go. I don't know how, but he had to be brought down. God gave me this land, and the mayor was not going to take it away from me. But what can I do? How can I fight such a powerful man? He's been connected with this local government for twenty years, mostly as mayor. He knows everybody, everything. I, on the other hand, have been in town only a few years and know no one, nothing. With no local friends or political background, what was I going to do?

It was an election year, and something had to be done, and it had to be done now. As if led by an invisible hand, I went to the municipal building and got the forms to run for mayor against Little Napoleon. I rushed home with the forms, dropped to my knees and prayed, "PLEASE, GOD, DON'T LET ME WIN." I had a lot of public sympathy, but I didn't want to be mayor. I just wanted to make change. I didn't know how I could accomplish it, but I knew I just could not sit back and do nothing.

The Borough Clerk told me how many names I needed on the petition, but I thought she was referring to residents. You have to remember that people in the municipal building were warned not to speak to me, consequently, they were afraid for their jobs and gave me little or no help at all when I decided to run for mayor. I got as many names as I could on the petition, mostly teenagers and elderly—everyone else was afraid of the mayor—but many names had to be crossed out because they were the opposite party or undeclared. What did I know? It's a good thing that I had more names than required, so my petition was accepted.

Then I noticed that political flyers had the name of a campaign manager at the bottom, so I figured I needed one, too. But I didn't know anyone in town. Besides, it was dangerous for anyone to be allied with me. They were afraid they would automatically inherit the wrath of the mayor and be subjected to harassment. I didn't want to put anyone's property or job in jeopardy. Then I remembered Elizabeth.

Elizabeth was an elderly German woman who spoke broken English and who was taking care of her even older sick husband. Her hands were full, so she had no time for local politics. I don't remember how I met this lady, perhaps in a local store, but she lived only a few blocks from me and would call me occasionally when she cooked one of her excellent German dishes.

Elizabeth was a safe choice for Campaign Manager. There is no way that the mayor would go after a senior citizen who is caring for a dying husband. How would that read in the newspaper? Elizabeth trusted me and signed the form. There really was no risk, as there was no money involved. She was just a name at the bottom of two flyers paid for by me. My total campaign—if you can call it that—came to about $650, two mailings. I later heard that the opposition spent a great deal of money, but I can't be sure what that figure was. When I look back at the whole thing, I have to laugh. It seems bizarre, now, for me to have run for mayor, but it was a desperate situation at the time.

Councilman Enters Race
Something unexpected and unprecedented happened. A councilman entered the race. He was the one who stomped out of the council meeting when I got up to make a statement about the Zoning Official, the one who said, "I don't have to listen to this!" We three presented a motley lineup for this affluent town: a short chain-smoking mayor who was like a short Edward G. Robinson, complete with cigar; a fat pompous councilman; and a scraggly lady piano tuner. I've seen better lineups than this in a grade B detective movie.

Poor Election Day Turnout
The Primary came upon us suddenly, and the next thing I knew, the polling machines were in place and the front door of the polling stations were wide open with huge arrows pointing the way. I kept reminding God that I don't want to win. I just want to get that Mayor out. I had no idea how this could possibly be accomplished.

On Election Day, the weather was not good. It was one of those cold damp miserable rainy days that made you want to stay home and keep warm. Also, the mayor's constituents were so over-confident that their four-term mayor would be a shoo-in, that very few came out. The poor voter turnout brought unexpected results.

The Tie
The Mayor and Councilman tied. I trailed behind. An astute politico who studied odds at elections the way gamblers do at Black Jack told me that had I gotten 35 more votes, I would have won. I didn't want to hear it. The very thought of winning made my head spin.

Despite my total lack of interest in this election, I was forced to be a part of the group that inspected the polling machines, after which we were all summoned to court to duke it out. They brought attorneys; I did not. I chose to sit in the audience, but the judge called me forward to sit with the Councilman and use his attorney to cover me. I don't know why I had to be a part of their battle.

Trial Results
The trial resulted in the Judge ordering a new election. I knew that the Mayor would be mobilizing his troops this time, and those shirkers who failed to vote the first time would now show up. The Councilman had very little going for him. He was nothing but a pawn on the council all these years. There was nothing spectacular about him. It was surprising that he found the muscle to run.

At this point, I felt that if I stayed in the race, I would be taking votes from the Councilman, not the Mayor. What I did was to step down and send a flyer to the town and urged all the residents who voted for me to vote for the Councilman. Residents would call me up and say, "But the councilman is so stupid." My answer to them was, "You got a choice here. Either you vote for Stupid or you vote for Evil." That seemed to take care of the problem. They voted for Stupid.

Most of my constituents were animal rights people who were incensed when there was an attempt on Lia's life. They knew who gave the orders. They did what I asked, and they voted for the Councilman. There must have been a lot of them, because the Councilman won the election, and it shocked the town.

It's Lonely At The Bottom

I got my final anonymous call from the polling station. The man said that the mayor just got the news that he lost the election, and he is standing there, in the middle of the near-empty hall, stunned and lifeless.

He told me that a disheartened constituent made his way slowly across the room up to the mayor and said, almost tearfully, "Mayor, why didja hafta bother the horse?"

CPSIA information can be obtained at www.ICGtesting.com
Printed in the USA
BVOW071012110112

280239BV00002B/4/P

9 781612 157887